# WEEDING
## THE GARDEN

# E. LEE JENSEN

authorHOUSE®

*AuthorHouse™*
*1663 Liberty Drive*
*Bloomington, IN 47403*
*www.authorhouse.com*
*Phone: 833-262-8899*



*Published by AuthorHouse  03/19/2021*

*ISBN: 978-1-6655-2054-6 (sc)*
*ISBN: 978-1-6655-2053-9 (e)*

*Print information available on the last page.*

*Any people depicted in stock imagery provided by Getty Images are models, and such images are being used for illustrative purposes only.*
*Certain stock imagery © Getty Images.*

*This book is printed on acid-free paper.*

**This is dedicated to**
**My loving Family**

# CONTENTS


Foreword...............................................................................................ix

1 - Is The Corona Virus Being Used To Kill Off The
Elderly And Aging ............................................................. 1
2 - Why our government wants to control our population .............. 13
3 - Why Social Security is broke in the United States ...................... 21
4 - Why our government might be conspiring against
us by using Covid-19 ........................................................... 25
5 - Body count rising as states hit their peaks, residents
ordered to stay and take shelter ......................................... 33
6 - The United States used Agent Orange chemicals
Against us in the 1960's, and 70's......................................... 37
7 - The United States Government conducted
Experiments On Its Own Citizens using Agent
Orange chemicals.................................................................. 43
8 - Donald J Trump stops funding to the World Health
Organization, for Covering up corona virus spread ..................... 49
9 - Elderly body count continuing amid corona virus cure............... 57
10 - Anonymous tip leads to 17 elderly bodies being
discovered in A make shift shed............................................. 59

11 - Democrats and social media misleading Covid-19
     cases to place blame on Trump ....................................... 63

12 - Is there a secret plot to damage Donald Trump and America? ... 69

13 - The hate agenda of the far left ...................................... 73

14 - The Democratic Party has no problems linking itself
     to known urban terrorist groups ................................. 77

15 - The more we know, The less we know ............................. 83

16 - The Food supply cut short among rising Covid-19 cases ............. 87

17 - The (C.D.C) Center for Disease Control now saying
     expect December To even be worse than current pandemic ....... 91

18 - Millions now hungry and unemployed ............................. 95

19 - The aging now have no place to go ................................ 97

20 - Was the corona virus devised to cost trump the Election? ........ 101

21 - Corona virus targets Trump voters aged 53 to 80 ..................... 103

About the Author ............................................................. 105

# FOREWORD

When I heard of this book being written, I jumped at the chance to write the foreword. Being 74 years old with heart trouble, I am a bold target for this virus. I am not some conspiracy nut, but this whole situation leads to many unanswered questions. Since when does a virus target a specific age group? Other than the elderly, it only attacks those that are already ailing, or those with a compromised immune system. Aside from the elderly, this virus is only fatal to a fraction of those that contract it and yet we in the U.S. are treating it like the Black Plague? We have a large homeless community that has not been touched by this virus, yet it takes hold in nursing homes?

I cannot believe any of the numbers being reported when each institution is awarded a bonus of $39,000 for recording a Corona virus death and only $13,000 dollars for listing the virus as a contributing factor. We saw the nursing home deaths reported in high numbers and we specifically read; 17 bodies found, 13 bodies found, etc.. How are they found? They certainly were not lost. If found dead, does this not indicate that these people were never sent to a hospital? Imagine watching these poor sick souls just languish and expire. Ask yourself, why would the nursing home miss out on their $39,000 bonus and give it to the hospitals? If it sounds sick……..it is. They had no incentive to provide these elderly patients with the best of care. What is with the blame game on where this virus originated? Was it an accident in a laboratory? Was it a bio-weapon being developed, was it from an animal? Was it from a Chinese Market? How at the base of this are Americans involved with Chinese scientists? Somehow all of our brainiac scientists have no idea and certain Politian's are left stuttering. All of us have to agree that this was totally exploited by our media. After getting orders to close businesses and be quarantined, the general public witnessed no significant effects and began ignoring the stay at home orders and protesting in masse.

I am usually pretty good at looking behind the curtain and seeing an answer, but this one confuses me. The only thing that really is damaged almost beyond repair is our economy? This was President Trumps crown and glory as he pulled our country back from Obama's legacy of sure financial ruin. Now, millions of Americans will lose their jobs, possibly their homes, and surely their dreams of a achievable bright future. It gets more scary when you realize that many other countries are jumping on the exterminate the elderly bandwagon. Without making this "short" forward into a chapter, countries made no secret of not wasting healthcare resources and just refusing to treat the elderly and just sending them home to die. Our country is discussing a Federal "DNR" law and overriding a person's healthcare wishes. Can all this be?? This book will certainly give you a lot to think about. If this was a conspiracy, it is a perfect one, leaving evidence pointing in all directions. All I know is at 74, I will no longer allow myself to be vaccinated or injected with anything anymore. I want what little time I have left regardless of whether the government views me as a unnecessary drag on the system. I worked my life paying into a retirement and healthcare system and it is owed to me. I will end this with a laugh. A year ago I looked into moving to a assisted senior facility which also is a nursing home. Only a day ago I received a phone call inviting me to have lunch with them. I said "Hell no!"

Edwin F. Becker, 2020

# CHAPTER ONE

## IS THE CORONA VIRUS BEING USED TO KILL OFF THE ELDERLY AND AGING

At the end of the day, we're all born as equals with our own lives to live. Each individual has their own stories to tell, their own uniqueness. At the end of the day governments are just made up of a group of humans who for some reason, Have come to think they can control the rest of us and brainwash us into what they feel we should be doing. Why can't they just live their own lives instead of focusing on dictating to others? What gives our government the right to decide who lives and who dies in this country? I thought only god made those decisions.

The entire world is on lockdown status, as a rampant killer virus wreaks havoc on what millions will say, has certainly changed their lives forever. Wuhan China is being secretive and the World Health Organization is being accused of covering up the spread of the virus pandemic. A virus I believe to be specifically designed to Weed The Garden. It seems the main focus is to Kill off the elderly and aging baby boomers of the world and to reduce the world's population.

I had never thought I would be the one truly believing in what some are calling a government cover-up, A conspiracy, that runs so deep it has become worldwide. However as a stone's fly here I am doing just that. I am still finding it difficult to sink my head into the thought, A concept so evil, that any government would want to kill off their elderly. It is a though that saddens me deeply. Everyone knows of someone who's getting up there in their older days or years, and most of us grew up with grandparents who were close to or over the age of sixty or seventy. Some of us may either be at that elderly level now or are nearing that age.

Our elder senior citizens all appear to be loving and caring, they are the true heroes, who have formed our society to date and should be protected at all costs. The elderly should never be targets in any shape or form. From recent news and media coverage it had been the topic for weeks. Now the topic all though nearly the same, has focused on the body counts of the deceased and much less on the surviving and survival rates. The one main topic is the continued cases and the fact it mainly has been the elderly losing their life.

The government now considers the dead as a statistical number that rings that surrender bell in my subconscious mind. It prepares me for the reality that man is out to kill humanity. Either through sure evilness or selfish greed, the fact is, it is now upon the entire world.

With pictures and videos of human beings being placed into plastic bags, I guess the right name used are body bags by the thousands, and the news media ramping up the death tolls worldwide. It makes perfect sense to be worried and to be afraid. I know I am. Despite the C.D.C and World Health Organizations both declassifying the actual virus spread as being less intensive then it should have. I for one have grown leery as to what they were never telling us in it's an entirety.

As you know we are facing a worldwide pandemic, one that has already killed hundreds of thousands globally. In our country alone, there is well over 600.000 cases of those that have caught the deadly virus, better known as Covid-19. A name China gave the virus with media stations around the world proudly displaying the news. The news coverage is always about the death count and how many have been infected by the virus. If scaring the world's population was not an agenda, they surely have done a great job at doing such. I also find it not hard to be stricken with despair, depression and at the same time, I can say that I am absolutely angry with The World Health Organization and the Center for Disease Control. After all, they have told people to not bother wearing masks. Then weeks later stated that it would be mandatory to wear masks. With people out there in our society, they are being traumatized to a point they do not know what to follow and or whom to follow. One would think some sort of twisted ploy was placed in to follow. Some sort of an informative action plan in place that had not benefited anybody.

This isn't a conspiracy, it is a Purge and it is happening as we write this book. For days I have single handedly watched as news agencies across the nation, and all over the world, from China to Italy and countries in between display their thoughts on the Corona virus and how it attacks the elderly and that the elderly is the main group with so many fatalities. Trying to understand why the elderly is been the main focus is beyond me. Many thoughts have come to mind, as why this virus is so rampant among the elderly? I could not help think this virus was some manmade virus to destroy the older population, and of course a few other casualties along the way. Maybe our government considers that casualties of doing business? I will call it the price of being elderly. the price of growing old.

Can it be just coincidence that for the past 3-5 years we have heard our government stating that the elderly are draining Social Security and increasing the cost of Medicare?

Day three hits and the media changes course yet again and states, if this virus spreads as it has, the media states there won't be enough hospital beds or respirators to help the sick and infectious virus patients. No shock there, but the media then counters and states that the elderly will be sent home and decisions will be made to who lives and who dies. The media on CNN and other news including Fox news local to where I live, states the elderly will have to take a back seat to the younger generations for a better chance of survival. Meaning the young will get treatment first. I sat there while listening to a segment and said to myself, this is a cleansing, this is a purge against anybody elderly, who may be sick or have the virus. This was totally not acceptable to me, nor should it be to anybody else either.

Growing up I was always taught to respect the elderly, to show dignity and have utter respect for those who have seen wars, and things we cannot possibly grasp. I guess being able to survive world wars and plagues and other diseases makes these people special and should be held as heroes to all. Not the media though, to the media, they are old used cargo that has to go. To make way for the young, or those said to be healthy. If this is the new world order I want no participation within it, or from it.

A recent story was aired on channel six news about a man living in Oregon, he had gotten the corona virus and survived, he was just 104 years old, had been in several wars and was also a national monument for the average American hero. If he can survive, so can many millions of elderly people. I see no reasoning, as to why we need to kill off anybody, let alone older people, other than that our social security system is near bankrupt and by killing off the elderly early, it can somehow make way for the young and a new retirement system. Think of all the money, that retirees have placed into their social security system. Then think of how many have abused that very same system making it dwindle to next to nothing?

Bill Lapschies has survived World War II, the 1918 flu, and now Coronavirus. He was one of the first people to be diagnosed with this virus in Oregon and has now recovered. In addition, he just turned 104 years old! Many are calling him an incredible survivor. I would say he is a big part of the cure for humanity's problem.......... a success story.

https://www.cbsnews.com/video/104-year-old-vet-recovers-from-Coronavirus-ju st-in-time-for-his-birthday/

We are hearing about one 104 year old man's fight and his remarkable journey through winning at odds with the Covid-19 virus and world pandemic, tears came to my eyes as I rejoiced that just maybe his story would show the entire world, 'that even the elderly had a chance to live. A chance as much as any young person would. After all, one person's life should never be traded for another and certainly not by some crooked political puppet either.

After weeks of hearing that socialized medicine was going to be applied and doctors would have to make decisions that affected our older generation, the ones society stated who would die and who could live. I began to wonder myself, if this was some Purge to simply dump the elderly at all costs. I kept reminding myself, it was the elderly that brought us to our levels that we are used to living at currently. Think about it. It was and elderly that fought in foreign wars for our freedoms and specific rights and freedoms and it was an elderly person that made prior inventions for us that we use daily and that list goes forward to fold.

With the CDC and the World Health Organization ramping up the hopelessness of the elderly and their survival rates, It even looked further, as if a complete breakdown of what I should call social injustice had begun to take place worldwide. At least in one country, Italy had begun to send home their elderly, stating they had no room for any more people. The hospitals were full and there were no other places to go. What they were really saying is if you are elderly go home and die in your home. Yes while the younger, yes the younger generation had began to get as much treatment, as they could. I do believe they called this socialized medicine. This is the part where they justify the killing of the elderly, or when they decide who lives and who does not. After days of seeing pictures from the heart of the Italian pandemic, body bags lined the streets, the Italian news sources along with American correspondents stated there was no room in morgues or freezers to house the bodies, so the government told them to leave the bodies in the street on the curb side for pick up. Again I wondered how many of them were senior citizens that the government decided to let them die in their homes? Keeping in mind, these people were someone's mother, somebody's father, sister a brother or what have you. They were not just numbers, but actual people whom needed more recognition then there countries gave them.

Doctors in Italy for instance were the first to rationalize the well being of millions of their elderly. The Italian government is rationing resources in their intensive care units amid the Coronavirus outbreak. Medical officials are urging health care workers not to treat elderly patients or patients with certain co morbidities, regardless of whether they have the virus. Another wards speaking of the disabled. They were told to play God and chose, who lived and or who gets a chance to live. With the elderly and I use this term closely with no ill will, already living on borrowed time. I cannot even begin to think, how they as a community of elders could even feel about even making their chances to survive that much less then what they may already have. To be honest, we are all living on borrowed time.

The Italian College of Anesthesia, Analgesia, Resuscitation and Intensive Care (SIAARTI) published utilitarian guidelines stating that doctors and nurses should deny treatment for people who have too low a number of expected "life-years" left. They advised hospitals to follow "the most widely shared criteria regarding distributive justice and the appropriate allocation of limited health resources." This includes ALL elderly patients needing intensive care treatment, not just those suffering from Coronavirus. Aged people with no signs of COVID-19 could be turned away at ICUs to clear space for younger patients who physicians perceive to have more "life-years" left and thus consider more worthy of investing medical resources. Again doctors playing god and deciding who lives and whom should die. What if all the elderly got together and decided it was the young who had to go first?

Italy, which alongside China has seen the bulk of Coronavirus cases, has now lost 11,000 from the outbreak. With the oldest population in

Europe due to the lowest fertility rate, Italy's elderly have suffered the heaviest toll. Instead of valuing the God-given dignity of the human person, the Italian health agency's new utilitarian guidelines degrade people to merely numbers and the elderly to absolute zero.

This outbreak unveils another layer of the disturbing utilitarian and discriminatory ideology of the culture of death, an ideology that the Pro-Life movement has fought long before Coronavirus. Texas Right to Life opposes policies that in letter or in effect discriminate against any patients or allow medical professionals to undervalue the neediest among us.

The worldwide panic and media hysteria caused by the Coronavirus is prompting people everywhere to neglect or disparage the elderly. Whether by words or deeds, anti-Life ethics have greatly influenced society's response to the disease. Undoubtedly, we cannot withdraw from our Pro-Life mission while trying to protect from the virus. Now is the time to respond with extraordinary compassion, level-headed caution, and uncompromising resolve to protect those most vulnerable. There is no doubt based on reports although very conflicting at times, it has been the elderly who have had to brave the storm and try to defend themselves from Covid-19.

The United States was fast to as they say, fast track a plan to also help out there failing social security and Medicare plan. Within a few days of Italy responding to their Virus crisis the USA also responded in similar manner with how the elderly are effected more so than anybody else and that most of them won't survive this Covid-19 virus. They stated in the media, that beds were filling up faster than capacity will allow. It was then they uttered the words of, "if push comes to shove, the doctors will have to take charge and make decisions on the patients amount of time left on this earth over a younger person who might live 60 years versus one with a ten year life expectancy left. Again the statements came as highly suspicious, as to the actual motives involved. Didn't they say in the near future in about 12 years, the social security system will be completely broke?

Keep in mind the news had stated on many different news segments all being said with a smile on their faces and laughter filling the news briefing. Either they were laughing because they were nervous, or because they were young and knew at least they might get treatment, if they became ill and or sick.

A Texas lieutenant governor hinted that the elderly can take care of themselves. USA ran the story. This same lieutenant governor of Texas argued in an interview on Fox News Monday night that the United States should go back to work, saying grandparents like him don't want to sacrifice the country's economy during the Coronavirus crisis. I think, he should be speaking for himself, because the elderly do not wish to die to please some back alley politician.

Republican Lt. Gov. Dan Patrick, 69, made the comments on Fox News' "Tucker Carlson Tonight" after President Donald Trump said he wanted to reopen the country for business in weeks, not months.

Patrick also said the elderly population, who the Centers for Disease Control and Prevention said are more at risk for COVID-19, can take care of themselves and suggested that grandparents wouldn't want to sacrifice their grandchildren's economic future. Sounds to me like the L.T governor was talking about the elderly dying to make way for the young?

"No one reached out to me and said, 'as a senior citizen, are you willing to take a chance on your survival in exchange for keeping the America that all America loves for your children and grandchildren?'" Patrick said. "And if that's the exchange, I'm all in." Even though Patrick had talked big, his ideology came up small.

"Patrick claimed after speaking to over a hundred people over the phone that there's a consensus that they don't want to "lose our whole country" over the current public health crisis and face an economic collapse. Why elderly people even entered his conversation, was clear and evident, that something was a foul. If there had been no conspiracy, it was adding up to be one.

Health experts have made clear the Coronavirus poses a particular danger for patients 60 years old and older – who face the highest risk of serious illness or death from the rapid spread of COVID-19. Health experts, have also been quick to write off the elderly, as if they are on borrowed time anyways. As I sit and get news updates from all over the world plus our local news stations, the chatter and talk is. What will they do when they run out of room in their freezers and hospital beds? Directly after that topic was quickly spoken about, came the message, that there will be some sort of program enforced on who exactly gets treated and who doesn't. No surprises there. After all this seems a governmental purge on the elderly and aging.

I noticed the other day when our census paperwork arrived that they stated it is against the law, if you do not fill it out. I was questioning the insensitive timing and or why they even bothered with their census, with all the recent deaths and this world pandemic and all. I wanted to believe it was just some coincidence and that relativity had no play in the recent paperwork. I mean what do I put there? Well our newborns gone he passed away do to virus and or Uncle Jack is gone, he also passed away knowing the government I basically feared the worst. I do think that the government has taught us to question and to fear the worst in whatever they tell us. Examples of this have been mapping up all over social media from live news coverage to websites that are allegedly dedicated to keeping the public updated and educated. Instead, they are purely frightening those I hold dearly the elderly. The elderly, are absolutely afraid to even leave there homes, they have been told over and over, if you get sick your dead.

What I simply have trouble with, is that our local news agency had talked about socialized medicine practices, but just today stated our governor will be giving respirators to the city of New York, as we are not in need of them right now. So what is it they planned on killing the elderly, but are not in need of the said ventilators after all? If this is so, then why even mention this. Why scare the elderly, what could be a purpose for this? I will tell you why, it is become a national ploy. The elderly have been and from the looks of it, will continue to be a national and state wide target during this national and world wide crisis.

The Florida Supreme Court wrote there is "a very legitimate concern that the "right to die" could become a license to kill," and that "there are times when some people believe that another would be "better off dead" even though the other person is still fighting vigorously to live. "Assisting the disabled and elderly to die" is just the thing needed by our society proclaim the "oh-so-wise" medical experts who go from county to county courthouse helping to make sure some disabled person gets killed with court approval.

And looking at the scorecard, some of the elderly and disabled are concluding they just may be better off dead. At least their despair of finding rescue from the dread conditions imposed upon them by our society, causes them to think that way. Hope for some is not forth coming and during this world pandemic, If the elderly do get sick, there futures looking poor, even worse than at times already though as being bad. With state wide statistics of one elderly in 3 will be abused, we cannot help wondering already, what do the elderly have to do, to even live as they should? With our governments economic collapse, this virus is a means to solve their fanatical issues and we have seen this on national television. It has been playing out like an old broken down record that is stuck on that continuous play mode.

To add salt to an already extreme situation, Washington State health leaders just this morning stated, they may be close to a cure, but under ordinary circumstances the cure might be more than a year out from public usage. Once again the news anchor asked, is there any way to speed that process up to help save maybe millions of lives? The answer came as no shock and in the way I had hoped it would not. What was described, is that the sick the ones who have been diagnosed with the virus and or the elderly, because they have a weakened immune system, would be the optimal ones for the said corona virus antidote or vaccine. The first thing that came to my thinking process was how come they only want to test the elderly? And what in the world is it with the constant beating of that elderly drum. It certainly seems obvious to me.

News just yesterday came in about a Tiger catching the corona virus. Fox news aired the story. A tiger and six other tigers fell ill in the Bronx zoo. It was one article that caught my attention. Now that it may be sad that a zoo animal is fallen ill it is also the first animal inside the USA to show that they too can catch this virus. It also shows that people, the elderly can take a back seat from socialized medicine because the scientists can infect the animal as the host and work on cures from that. I did not see anything mentioned by either the World Health authority or any other disease centers on using the animals infected as test patients to better find a cure. You won't either.

https://www.fox4news.com/news/tiger-at-nyc-bronx-zoo-positive-for-Coronaviru  s?fbclid=IwAR2r7jj1r4u6rN5sOSLBu54aBt-enUjRSmHJPAZktxptmHXIg7Z_QQClpYQ

From the beginning of this Corona scare, pandemic, whatever you wish to label it, the disease centers had mentioned that animals can also get the virus. Just why aren't they using them to help all humanity then? that answer is relatively easy, why should they when they can lower the elderly population and use them instead. It is called population control. Population control happens when the government is in fear of overpopulation. It is also called **WEEDING THE GARDEN.**

# CHAPTER TWO

## WHY OUR GOVERNMENT WANTS TO CONTROL OUR POPULATION

**P**opulation control, or more specifically human population control, is a term that usually refers to various national government programs and policies that aim to slow the growth of a country's population. Common population control methods enacted in various countries can include restricting how many children each family is allowed to have, forced sterilizations, increased availability of contraceptives, and education about methods of birth control. Encouraging emigration and restricting immigration are other ways for a country to slow its population growth. The reason for trying to curb population growth with these methods is usually a fear of current or future overpopulation, which is thought to lead to famine and poverty. Many believe that overpopulation both globally and in a specific country can lead to environmental and economic problems if there are more people than can be sustained by the available resources. Sustainable resources, usually means one specific thing, that being monetary or money. Keep in mind, Money is the new evil.

In this case without economic relief, we cannot continue to support the elderly, social security and rising costs of health care. In this regard it might make sense to target the elderly and by the looks of how this pandemic has surfaced through the media to be exactly what the plan was. To control the population through socialized medicine.

Some methods of population control rely on voluntary participation, for example by offering economic incentives to those choosing to have fewer children, or offering free sterilizations or easily obtained birth control. Other government policies can be punitive, including fines or other forms of punishment if a family has more than the allowed number of children. Punitive measures can also include forcing pregnant women to undergo abortions, or forcing men and women to be sterilized. Such involuntary forms of population control are controversial, considered by many to violate human rights, and are not commonly part of the official policy in any country. Consider the fact that the United States has approved late term abortions and even killing a live baby should it survive. Can anyone dispute that drastic steps at population control are a priority?? If they would allow killing infants, what chance do the elderly have?

Some scientists argue that world population control is essential for humanity's long-term survival, economically and environmentally. They believe that humanity will deplete the Earth's resources if the global population continues to increase. Other scientists believe that the fears of global overpopulation are overstated, and that population growth does not have to be detrimental to the environment or the economy.

August 17, 2015 (POP) — Contrary to the fear mongering of the population alarmists, the world isn't heading for a demographic catastrophe. The latest data on world population from the U.N. Population Division reveals a number of trends that seem to indicate otherwise. The following is PRI's brief overview of some of the findings from the recently released 2015 Revision of the World Population Prospects.

Population alarmist would have us believe the world is overpopulated with too many people placing too great a strain on the environment and our resources. While it is true that we all share limited resources on this one planet we call home, hunger and poverty in the world today are largely the result of underdevelopment, civil strife or conflict, and poor distribution of wealth, not an excess in today's population. Environmental degradation, although a pressing problem, has much more to do with an irresponsible disposal of waste, corporations cutting corners to meet their bottom lines, poor urban planning and excessive urban sprawl, and a culture of waste that has been fostered in developed nations.

In an article written by Prepper News on July 16,2019,the article stated" Population control is probably coming to America. NBC news, the Royal family, and a number of other sources, were also pushing population control strategies in America. At the prior time, I myself began to wonder why all the sudden these topics had come to surface and why the media had so feverishly broadcasted such information. It was as if there was some strategy already in place, some sort of what I would call conspiracy. Was it a said strategy to void the Earth or United States of hundreds of thousands or millions of human lives, was this some sort of planned killing of the Earth's population worldwide?

NBC News blatantly stated that population control was needed in order to save the planet. This all went down or happened about the same time this flu came to surface, or what doctors had called the flu and had so many cases, they were simply sending people home. It's the flu, go home and call your doctors, is what was being told to millions, the doctors stated it is a super bad cold and flu season, but I knew it was much more than that.

China had stated in several news reports, that the United States had created the agenda of this corona virus and that The United States had blamed them, when the American Army had created it. They also stated the Army had released the Corona Virus Covid-19.

After reading about two top notch Nano scientists being arrested, that were attached to Harvard University and their biological program, I almost assuredly suspected something was going on and the F.B.I. was not talking. On January 28th,2020 Harvard head of chair, professor, D.R Charles Lieberman Was arrested and charged with espionage, or making false statements to the State department about receiving funds directly from China. When Lieberman was arrested, news circulated around the country and was on nearly everyone's conspiracy pages, that followed such things. Truth is. Whatever Lieberman was working on, there said funding did come from the alleged center of the corona virus Covid-19 and Wuhan China. It had been said Lieberman, was getting 50,000 a month and other fees for his work. It was also stated other's stood to profit millions of dollars.

With our very liberal television news agencies and our democrats focusing on population control, We should have begun to realize, we may have a serious problem on our hands. It had seemed as if it went unnoticed for a while, at least until this virus miraculously appeared, thus killing tens of thousands around the world. People began falling ill and deaths started being reported hourly from state to state and in every country, it was the same.

Millionaire Pennsylvanian, Scott Wallace, with millions in donations, contributed to population control groups such as Zero Population, Growth/ Population Connection and some others. His donations and his power in politics, placed a different perspective, for those paying attention. The agenda then, was population control. If the elderly population got any concept of what Scott Wallace may have been planning, they did not let anyone else in on that said secret.

From the very beginning, the concept of a "population explosion" was an ideologically motivated false alarm specifically designed to allow rich nations to pillage the resources of the poorer nations. NSSM-200 represents the worst aspect of the "advanced" nations meddling in the most intimate affairs of less-developed nations. It reinforces the image of the "ugly American." It advocates violating the most precious freedoms and autonomy of the individual through coercive family planning programs.

Tens of billions of dollars of government population control expenditures have accomplished is to make hundreds of millions of large families, poor families into smaller poor families. It is unfortunately left to our imagination to wonder what might have happened if these resources had been invested in health and educational infrastructure, and in research dedicated to finding peaceful strategies to transition nations from corrupt governance to truly representative and accountable courts and public service sectors.

It is a well known fact China has over population problems inside their own countries. Chinas population is 1,438,76,420, with a baby being born less then every second. 1 in every 10 people are elderly in china, with nearly 132 million elderly or aging. China's famous one-child policy had an aftereffect of creating a larger elderly population. Westerners often hear about how much regard the Chinese have for the elderly, but as China grows old, a number of challenges potentially await the emerging superpower. With this review of the elderly in China, better your understanding of how old people are treated in the country and the impact of a rapidly aging population.

Since more and more elderly live alone, homes for the elderly aren't enough to meet their needs. One report found that Beijing's 289 pension houses could accommodate only 9,924 people or 0.6 percent of the population above age 60. To better serve the elderly, Beijing adopted regulations to encourage private and foreign investment in "homes for the elderly."

Some officials believe that the problems facing China's elderly can be solved through combined efforts from family, the local community, and society as a whole. China's goal is to establish a support network for senior citizens that provides medical care and helps them avoid loneliness through scholarly pursuits and entertainment. The network would also encourage senior citizens to continue serving society after retirement age by using the knowledge they've acquired over the years.

As China's population ages, the nation will also have to take a hard look at how this shift will affect its ability to compete on the world stage. China is not unique in needing to consider the treatment of its elderly population.

The United States is in no better position, with a failed social security system among other supposed structured elderly and health care programs you have to wonder, has this covid-19 been used to exploit the countries' economic system. Did Democrats and even the said queen of England have anything to do with this so called pandemic? After all this it surely seems entirely probable. Whatever the case may be, somebody knows something and the American people are without explanations and or answers.

Rather than diminish the fear that inspires humans to act in irrational violent ways, philosophy professor Peter Ludlow writes that so-called democracies are using it as a weapon to "control the rabble." Events such as 9/11 and other terrorist acts have been framed and used constantly as a justification of an ever-growing surveillance state that is backed by our political leaders. After a distressing, must-read litany of the many ways in which American citizens have forfeited their liberties out of fear, Ludlow offers some hope. "Yet ultimately we are not powerless," he writes. "We can resist the impulse to be afraid." Being afraid is perhaps one of the greatest understatements of all time.

The United States National Security Council is the highest decision-making body on foreign policy in the United States. On December 10, 1974, it promulgated a top secret document entitled National Security Study Memorandum or NSSM-200, also called The Kissinger Report. The subject was "Implications of Worldwide Population Growth for U.S. Security and Overseas Interests." This document, published shortly after the first major international population conference in Bucharest, was the result of collaboration among the Central Intelligence Agency (CIA), the United States Agency for International Development (USAID), and the Departments of State, Defense and Agriculture.

The Kissinger Report was made public when it was declassified and was transferred to the U.S. National Archives in 1990. Although the United States government has issued hundreds of policy papers dealing with various aspects of American national security since 1974, The Kissinger Report continues to be the foundational document on U.S. government population control.

In order to protect U.S. commercial interests, NSSM-200 cited a number of factors that could interrupt the smooth flow of materials from LDCs to the United States, including a large population of anti-imperialist youth, whose numbers must be limited by government population control. The document identified 13 nations by name that would be the primary targets of U.S. government population control efforts. Under the heading of "Concentration on key countries" we find:

The document has directly and inevitably encouraged atrocities on an enormous scale in dozens of the world's nations. Just four examples are shown below. China. For many years, the United States government funded the United Nations Population Fund (UNFPA). In April 2017, Peru. During the years 1995 to 1997, over a quarter of a million Peruvian women were sterilized as part of a program to fulfill then-president Alberto Fujimori's family planning goals.

Uganda. Uganda became the first African country to roll back its adult HIV infection rate, from 21% in 1991 to about 6% in 2004, a 70% decrease. The nation accomplished this amazing feat by discouraging condom use and by changing the behavior of the people. The population control groups could not allow this success to interfere with their inflexible template, so they aggressively undermined President Yoweri Museveni's program. Timothy Wirth, president of the United Nations Foundation, called this highly effective program "gross negligence toward humanity"

India. In 2014 there was renewed international attention on India's continuing forced sterilization program after dozens of women were killed and many more harmed due to the assembly line procedures being done in grotesquely unsanitary conditions. Female sterilization is still India's primary method of "contraception." According to the New York Times, as of 2016 four million tubal ligations are still done annually. This continues to be financed by the US and other Western governments and foundations. As of 2017 there are no plans to stop sterilizations, but the Indian government is introducing free inject-able contraceptives, which will also have major negative health impacts on women.

Throughout the implementation process, the United States must hide its tracks and disguise its government population control programs as altruistic: There is growing awareness that the world "population explosion" is over or, indeed, that it never actually materialized. When the population scare began in the late 1960s, the world population was increasing at a rate of more than 2% per year. It is now increasing at less than one percent per year, and this rate is expected to continue to drop due to continuing population control activities.

The Kissinger Report predicted that the population of the world would stabilize at about 10 to 13 billion, with some demographers predicting that the world population would balloon to as high as 22 billion people. Now it is estimated that by 2050 population will level out at around 9.7 billion.

With this new pandemic nobody knows if population control is needed, or how many millions will lose their lives due to this virus spread and contamination worldwide.

What we do know for sure, is that The United States has actively engaged with the help of The United Nations with population control already, so it makes sense, that they would be quite eager to have some sort of population control in the U.S.A as well.

From the very beginning, the concept of a "population explosion" was an ideologically motivated false alarm specifically designed to allow rich nations to pillage the resources of the poorer nations. The resulting push for population control in LDCs has borne absolutely no positive fruit in its decades of implementation. In fact, population control ideologies and programs make it even more difficult to respond to the impending grave crisis looming in the form of a disastrous worldwide "population implosion." **It is time to begin urging families to have more children, not less, if we are to avoid a worldwide demographic catastrophe.**

# CHAPTER THREE

## WHY SOCIAL SECURITY IS BROKE IN THE UNITED STATES

You've undoubtedly heard this question asked - maybe you've even participated in some discussions on the topic. So is Social Security really going bankrupt? The answer to that question might depend mostly on your personal circumstances. If you are currently relying on Social Security income, or you will be in the next few years, it's a question you don't even want to entertain. But if you're many years away from retirement, it might be a foregone conclusion that it won't be there when it's your turn. I am 53 and I doubt it will be there even when I officially retire.

When you take a closer look at an already admitted failing social security fund, you need to take a look at the proposals to fix them. Oh there has been ideas generated and ideas passed around during election times, but the only logical conclusion, could be to simply kill off the elderly. If the elderly pass away and especially those just before retirement, it would consistently change the dynamics of this faltering social security system.

The retirement of the 76 million-member Baby Boom Generation is only the most obvious problem. Less discussed is the Social Security Disability benefits.

As most retirees and soon-to-retirees already know, Social Security is slated to run out of money in 2034 and, unless changes are made between now and then, beneficiaries beginning in that year will receive only 79% of what they otherwise would be owed. That is if there is even any money to use for our retirees and elderly folks applying for social security.

To be sure, predicting what will come out of Congress in the next few months is an inexact science at best, much less the next 15 years. But if anyone can gauge Social Security's real-world prospects, it should be Andy Landis, author of "Social Security: The inside Story". Landis, for those of you who don't know him, is a former Social Security Administration representative who has several decades of experience explaining the intricacies of Social Security to retirees and soon-to-be-retirees.

We are now fast approaching the unsustainable reality that there are barely two working people paying taxes to support the benefits being paid to each Social Security recipient. As that equation continues to deteriorate, the situation becomes increasingly unbalanced.

And politics aside, the financial industry stands to benefit from the hysteria as well. Public fears over the annihilation of Social Security makes for excellent marketing fodder when you're trying to hawk retirement plans and other investment products.

With The United States government so deeply in debt, they are faced with a drastic decision to either balance an already pre-bankrupt of the social security system, or to find another way to do so. This is what makes us wonder about this virus Covid-19. Considering the fact other countries, they to have a population issue, it is not hard to wonder if Covid-19 was designed to one create a population decrease as well as fix our ailing social security system. Keep in mind when one social security client dies it is that much less to the burden of that already defunded social security system. Make no mistake about it, it is killing off the elderly......... One by one.

In November, nearly 62 million people received a benefits check from the Social

Security Administration via the Old Age, Survivors, and Disability Insurance Trust (OASDI). About 42.4 million of these recipients were retired workers. As the number of retirees continues to grow, the importance of this monthly stipend that Social Security provides will as well.

According to the Social Security Administration, 62% of all retired workers count on their Social Security check to provide at least half of their monthly income, with 34% of retired beneficiaries leaning on the program for between 90% and 100% of their total income. Though Social Security was designed as a supplementary income source for lower-income folks during retirement, it's transformed into a nest egg in and of itself over the past couple of decades.

But this source of retirement income is on thin ice, at least according to the latest report from the Social Security Board of Trustees. Per the 2017 Trustees report, the OASDI will begin paying out more in benefits than it's generating in annual revenue by 2022. Just 12 years after that, in 2034, the OASDI is expected to have completely exhausted its $3 trillion in asset reserves.

In 2016, $957.5 billion in revenue was collected for Social Security. Nearly $33 billion of this came from the taxation of Social Security benefits. It isn't the first time social security received enough funds to sustain it for decades, so where has all the social security funding gone then? If you asked the government, they are going to blame the elderly population and prior baby boomers.

If you're worried about the long-term viability of Social Security, you're not alone. Writes C.B.S news in Early June of 2018. According to a recent report by the Transamerica Center for Retirement Studies, more than three-fourths (76 percent) of American workers fear that Social Security won't be there for them when they're ready to retire. This concern spans generations, expressed by 65 percent of baby boomers, 80 percent generation-X's and 83 percent of millennia's.

The scary headlines result from the "2018 Social Security Trustees Report" that was released in early June, which showed virtually no change in the program's long-term deficit. According to the report, the long-term actuarial deficit is 2.84 percent of payroll, compared to 2.83 percent in the 2017 report.

This means some combination of benefit adjustments and tax increases with a total value of 2.84 percent of worker's aggregate compensation could put the program into long-term actuarial balance. This is a doable goal, if our political leaders can find the will to reach acceptable compromises that address the system's funding problems. The problem arising is that there has been no compromising and no true efforts to establish a safety net to protect the almost bankrupt system.

On June 5 the Social Security Trustees released their 2018 report on the financial status of the federal government's largest program, which levies the largest tax most workers pay and which provides the biggest share of most retirees' incomes. And for the most part the Report showed a holding pattern: no big changes, except the passage of a year means we're one year closer to the Social Security trust funds' insolvency. And that's the bad news, because **our seniors and aging will be out of luck and out of money.**

# CHAPTER FOUR

## WHY OUR GOVERNMENT MIGHT BE CONSPIRING AGAINST US BY USING COVID-19

I hate to be pessimistic, but I've learned over time that the US government lies or conceals nearly everything that it is not forced to disclose. Even when it is compelled to disclose information, stall tactics are employed because 'time heals all wounds' or at least makes the information irrelevant. If disclosure can be delayed by months or years, many layers of headlines will have dulled the public appetite for the information, leaving actors in government free to act unconstrained in the meantime. That is just the small part of the government and that is the problem, not knowing, what is truth and what is not the truth. It has gotten so bad, that as a people, we don't trust our politicians, we don't trust media outlets and news sources any longer.

Let me start by pointing out that most all our nation's vital statistics have declined significantly over the last 50 years or so. The underlying reason is that somewhere in the late 1960's private interests began to take precedence over social concerns in the affairs of government, creating a fundamental shift in the paradigm that determines our nation's policies. As our representatives became more beholding to special interests, they found it increasingly necessary to hide their abandonment of public interests, which has led to their current reputation of being among the most distrusted people in our country. Incredible and perhaps cynical as it may sound, the reality is that our government now lies to us about virtually everything. Because must they know all answers to various special interests, when our representatives address their purpose is not to inform the people, but rather to manipulate public opinion. The next time you hear a news person talking about or to a politician, ask yourself if it's about informing or manipulating the public. We have become so immune to the practice of politicians not simply speaking the truth, but rather carefully crafting their statements to steer public opinion that we scarcely notice that that's all they do.

We have so many cover-ups because government has become more about selling the control that can ensure private success, than doing that which serves the needs of the people.

I have done tons of reading. I have read numerous commission reports, including the 911 and Warren commission reports, and from all indications, we (the US public) are being lied to constantly. I have come to the inescapable conclusion that our government is totally and utterly incapable of telling the public the truth, so I am completely and utterly incapable of believing anything they say. The Obama presidency and the FBI handling of Hilary's email scandal shredded any minute credibility the government had left.

If a government shares a piece of knowledge with the people of the nation, they have shared that knowledge with everybody in the world. There is no way that any nation engaging in international trade or finance, whose scholars participate in international conferences, or whose vacationers travel internationally will be able to keep all these people from saying things that will alert others to the secret. The only way to do it would be for the nation to act like North Korea, and keep the vast majority of its people in the dark, figuratively and literally. I think, we can all understand, that some secrets must remain classified and just that……..Kept secret.

Where Covid-19 is concerned, we have all been told that it was a virus, that escalated from one animal through another and then from that animal to a human. A Bat, they had notified the world. after weeks and in review, the said virus took on an entirely different program, perhaps like it was designed to and then hundreds of elderly people began to start dying one by one. The fact is our government from day 1 has told the American public, that this virus started in Wuhan China at some fish market. According to Chinese state media, researchers at a South China Agricultural University have analyzed over 1,000 met-genome samples of wild animals to find pangolins, a type of anteater, are the most likely intermediate host of the novel Coronavirus.

Shen Yongyi, a professor with the university and member of the research team, told the Xinhua news service that although previous research found the novel Coronavirus originated in bats, the animals hibernate in winter, making it unlikely that they caused the current outbreak.

"The evidence for the potential involvement of pangolins in the outbreak had not been published, other than by a university press release," said Professor James Wood, PhD, Head of Department of Veterinary Medicine, University of Cambridge in a statement. "This is not scientific evidence; investigations into animal reservoirs are extremely important, but results must then be published for international scrutiny to allow proper consideration. Simply reporting detection of viral RNA with sequence similarity of >99 percent is not sufficient." I would tend to agree.

As the so called spread of the Corona virus, the virus had mutated and went another direction with a more severity then the first undulated strain. This creating some uncertainty, as to what the Corona virus actually was.

As the Wuhan fish market story began to make its rounds, more and more people were becoming skeptic, as to the reported authenticity of the Wuhan market report, and as far as it being accurate. The entire story seemed to be missing something. Can we say something was fishy? The American public, for the most part, has come to the idea, that if our governments telling a story, it is either over inflated or under inflated, meaning wishy-washy every single time.

It has been well documented in time, that our government has lied to us all and it seems as if that is a misguided statement, but reality has shown us, that perhaps we have to use our own judgment when it is needed to weed out the phony untrue facts from the harsh reality of everyday life.

As the world tries to put every resource into containing the outbreak, one question continues to puzzle scientists: Where did the new Coronavirus come from?

New evidence suggests that humans may not have picked up the virus from Wuhan's infamous wet market. The latest study of the first 366 children who caught the infection in early January found no connection to the market. While there is enough evidence to prove that the virus jumped from animals — bats to an intermediary animal and then to humans — scientists do not know where the virus took hold. China alerted the World Health Organization (WHO) of a pneumonia-like illness circulating in Wuhan. It did not take long for scientists from China to release the genetic information of the virus.

The first clue stemmed from a study that looked at the first 41 hospitalized patients in Wuhan. Something stood out in the data: 13 of the first 41 patients had nothing to do with the Hunan market. What the last 13 did have to do with the Covid disease, was they were infected.

To understand that, scientists play detective as they try to identify the first few COVID-19 patients. This is proving to be a challenge given that the virus moved discreetly. This is not the only study. According to researchers from Xishuangbanna Tropical Botanical Garden under the Chinese Academy of Sciences and the Chinese Institute for Brain Research, the virus was brought into the market from elsewhere. The market, in turn, may have helped the virus spread and circulate efficiently. However I do not believe it was the original place of infection.

From the data, they found that the virus may have been moving among people in late November or early December. "The genomic evidence did not support the Huanan market as the birthplace of SARS-CoV-2,

In January the F.B.I arrested a top Harvard Nano scientists and three other people, on then suspected espionage, that did have direct links to the Chinese laboratory and research center in Wuhan China, was this a coincidence? I think not, even though the government, was definitely telling the world, that the cases had no link and they were correct, the charges had no link to Covid officially, but the research center, where the virus was said to have originated from, certainly did and so did the exact same city and town Wuhan China.

Finding a child who developed the disease outside of Wuhan in the early days of the outbreak suggests, "it didn't just start in a fish market," Dr. Matthew B. Frieman, from the University of Maryland School of Medicine, tweeted. I had to agree with them.

Chinese scientists believe the deadly Coronavirus may have started life in a research facility just 300 yards from the Wuhan fish market. A new bombshell paper from the Beijing-sponsored South China University of Technology says that the Wuhan Center for Disease Control (WHCDC) could have spawned the contagion in Hubei province. The possible origins of 2019-nCoV Coronavirus,' penned by scholars Botao Xiao and Lei Xiao claims the WHCDC kept disease-ridden animals in laboratories, including 605 bats.

It also mentions that bats – which are linked to Coronavirus – once attacked a researcher and 'blood of bat was on his skin.'

The report says: 'Genome sequences from patients were 96% or 89% identical to the Bat CoV ZC45 Coronavirus originally found in Rhinolophus affinis (intermediate horseshoe bat).'

It describes how the only native bats are found around 600 miles away from the Wuhan seafood market and that the probability of bats flying from Yunnan and Zhejiang provinces was minimal.

In addition there is little to suggest the local populace eat the bats as evidenced by testimonies of 31 residents and 28 visitors.

Pictures had surfaced over the past few weeks of the Wuhan wet market selling of bats and other lizards, it had created a false pretense, that the wet market, was actually the culprit for the rare and undocumented virus. Social media, helped spread the alleged sources of the virus, even though unfounded at that time. The U.S government did nothing to combat the story and allowed that story to play out worldwide and that it has done.

Another article appears. The article explains more clearly that the Wuhan version of the virus could have come only from the US because it is what they call a "branch" which could not have been created first because it would have no 'seed'. It would have to have been a new variety spun off the original 'trunk', and that trunk exists only in the US. (1)

Let the conspiracy theories roll. if you use your thinking cap and actually gather all the intelligence that you can find, if you are careful the entire situation seemed as if we blamed china and China blamed us, but what if both the United States and China were both the culprits for this virus. We have been told that this virus has some 14 day incubation period, where the systems don't show for at least two weeks. What if in the said beginning that was a much longer time. If this was plausible, then the United States theory could very well be correct. It is very difficult to tell, because both governments will lie there teeth off. Our government lied about Roswell they have also lied about the JFK conspiracy, as everyone knew there were multiple shooters, three shots fired and from different directions. The point is, if we could get them to stop lying, we might be able to fully understand, exactly what has happened. The truth is, our government and foreign governments lie to us daily. It is what they do.

One said theory was If some members of the US team at the World Military Games that were held (18-27 October) had become infected by the virus from an accidental outbreak at Fort Detrick it is possible that with a long initial incubation period, their symptoms might have been minor, and those individuals could easily have 'toured' the city of Wuhan during their stay, infecting potentially thousands of local residents in various locations, many of whom would later travel to the seafood market from which the virus would spread like wildfire (as it did). However that is just a theory, that the Wuhan government would like to accredit to the United States. It is certainly something to keep in mind.

As the Virus origin became even more under scrutiny one paper wrote""As confirmed cases of a novel virus surge around the world with worrisome speed, all eyes have so far focused on a seafood market in Wuhan, China, as the origin of the outbreak. But a description of the first clinical cases published in The Lancet on Friday challenges that hypothesis. " This is what supports and sort of makes one's mind think there could be much more to the story.

This would provide impetus for caution among the public in accepting the "official standard narrative" that the Western media are always so eager to provide – as they did with SARS, MERS, and ZIKA, all of which 'official narratives' were later proven to have been entirely wrong.

In this case, the Western media flooded their pages for months about the COVID-19 virus originating in the Wuhan seafood market, caused by people eating bats and wild animals. All of this has been proven wrong. We as a world population know damned well, that china has had a laboratory no less than 600 feet away from the wet market. A research market that worked with germ warfare and biological agents of mass destruction.

Based on the new information and factual truth now being told, it seems either our government knew where the suggested source came from or was naïve in finding the truth. I would have to think, they knew all along what was what and that somehow was a special part of this biological weapon

The TV Asahi network presented scientific documentation for their claims, raising the issue that no one would know the cause of death because the US either neglected to test or failed to release the results. Japan avoided the questions of natural vs. man-made and accidental vs. deliberate, simply stating that the virus outbreak may first have occurred in the US. The Western Internet appears to have been scrubbed of this information, but the Chinese media still reference it.

The basic logic is that the geographical location with the greatest diversity of virus strains must be the original source because a single strain cannot emerge from nothing. A recent scientists from Taiwan have demonstrated that only the US has all the five known strains of the virus (while Wuhan and most of China have only one, as do Taiwan and South Korea, Thailand and Vietnam, Singapore, and England, Belgium and Germany), constituting a thesis that the heliotypes in other nations may have originated in the US. If this is so, then The United States, either by accidental exposure or by deliverance has had a great deal to do with the said virus. It also leads much suspicion to the United States Army's closing of their biological lab in January.

According to some scientists, the virus would have to be a compile of both the virus from China and the said viruses from the United States. The Taiwanese doctor then stated the virus outbreak began earlier than assumed, saying, "We must look to September of 2019".

He stated the case in September of 2019 where some Japanese traveled to Hawaii and returned home infected, people who had never been to China. This was two months prior to the infections in China and just after the CDC suddenly and totally shut down the Fort Detrick bio-weapons lab claiming the facilities were insufficient to prevent loss of pathogens.

The truth is I believed some virus warfare had already gotten out, or the virus was breached or stolen and that problem had alerted the C.D.C into closing the United States based laboratory. We can add all the what-If's and most likely never fully get the entire picture, as to what exactly happened. What we must understand, is that the entire world is changed as we randomly go about our daily lives. We now must live in fear, and in our minds think, are we next? **Will we survive and unseen enemy?**

# CHAPTER FIVE

## BODY COUNT RISING AS STATES HIT THEIR PEAKS, RESIDENTS ORDERED TO STAY AND TAKE SHELTER

With the body count rising and the death toll multiplying, there seems to be no mercy for the ones who have either battled the deadly virus, or the victims who fell to Covid-19. Every state in The United States is now declaring a national and state emergency, the pandemic as it is being called, is now out of control. Casualties of an unseen enemy now lurk in our homes, in our work places and of course in elderly homes, who seem to be the most vulnerable to it. The absolute worst part is, it is on all of our minds and even in our dreams.

Sir Patrick Vallance, the country's top scientist, said the number of people who die from Covid-19 will continue to go up after infections reach their height. Asked about how long he expected to see deaths continue to rise, Sir Patrick said: "In general, I'd expect the deaths to keep going up for about two weeks after the intensive care picture improves.

Sir Patrick said for that reason it is important to continue with the measures that are currently in place. I had to sit down and think to myself, what are those measures exactly? To stay at home, to not have contact with people, our own loved ones? Whatever the restrictions were, we had to know that huge sacrifices would be hard to deal with and still overcome.

England confirmed the latest victims were aged between 24 and 103, including 43 with no underlying health conditions. The latest figure means the total number of deaths in England is now at 7,248.

The Maryland Department of Health announced further information on the 11 deaths Saturday evening. Four of the deaths were residents of Prince George's County, with two men in their 50s, one in his 60s and a woman in her 70s.

There have now been more than 2.5 million confirmed cases of Coronavirus globally, with more than 60,000 deaths. There have been more than 278,000 cases, and 7,100 deaths, in the United States alone. As these numbers continued to grow, so did skepticism that a cure was to be found any time soon.

A key concern among public health officials is a surge in cases that overwhelms hospitals and other healthcare facilities. Those hit hardest by the virus need intensive care, and sometimes ventilators, which are in short supply. This has created an automatic death sentence for those needing respirators and not being able to get them. To the government, they are statistical numbers and when it comes down to it, less important than others.

**The death count continues to rise:**

But Americans appear to be losing interest, at least as measured by Google Trends data. Searches related to Coronavirus have been declining in the US since the end of January. The US has 53 confirmed cases, including 36 people who were on the quarantined Diamond Princess, cruise ship in Japan.

The decline in interest could be because the outbreak appears to be stabilizing within China — the World Health Organization said on Monday that the epidemic peaked and plateaued there between January 23 and February 2. Similarly, a recent study of more than 72,000 Coronavirus patients in China found that the largest number of patients were showing symptoms on February 1,2020

But the virus' international spread may be getting worse. Coronavirus cases have been reported in 34 other countries, and 33 people have died internationally. South Korea has been hardest hit — the WHO confirmed 602 Coronavirus cases and five deaths there on Sunday.

Italy has at least 215 reported cases and six deaths. It's unclear how some of those patients became ill. On Monday, a dozen towns in Italy were placed on lockdown.

In Iran, meanwhile, the Coronavirus outbreak has forced schools to close. Officials initiated a campaign to disinfect public places after 43 people got sick and 12 died.

The most disruptive thing to hit markets in many years' is the Corona Virus. Financial experts, began to worry about their investments. The Dow plummets 5,000 points, erases gains for the year, as Coronavirus fears rattle traders and to make things worse

Vietnam is set to lose billions of dollars due to the Coronavirus, and it's already feeling the impact of the deadly outbreak, to add a little more to it a South Vietnamese bar in Ho Chi Minh City bans Chinese customers, as Coronavirus concerns spark anti-Chinese racism. Even our own country began to show racism to Chinese people after the media notified the entire world that the virus had been because of a Wuhan Wet market.

The infamous Dow plummets 5,000 points, erases gains for the year, as Coronavirus fears rattle traders.

At first the United States, was the first one to place the said blame on China and that made me look to another cause. As a kid I had remembered playing the name game and as I remembered, **it was always the person speaking the loudest, who was at fault.**

# CHAPTER SIX

## THE UNITED STATES USED AGENT ORANGE CHEMICALS AGAINST US IN THE 1960'S, AND 70'S

If you were to ask the government why they used Agent Orange on our own service men, they would say it was to help get rid of the foliage, so the enemy could not hide, but what perhaps they should have told everybody, was that it was an experiment that eventually went bad in Vietnam, Thailand and of course The United States. So exactly what is Agent Orange used for? Chemical warfare of course.

Agent Orange is a herbicide and defoliant chemical, one of the "tactical use" Rainbow Herbicides. It is widely known for its use by the U.S. military as part of its chemical warfare program, Operation Ranch Hand, during the Vietnam War from 1961 to 1971. It is a mixture of equal parts of two herbicides, 2,4,5-T and 2,4-D. In addition to its damaging environmental effects, traces of dioxin (mainly TCDD, the most toxic of its type) found in the mixture have caused major health problems for many individuals

Agent Orange was used in a number of military operations during the 1960s and 1970s. Though most commonly associated with Vietnam, it surely isn't the first time a chemical had been used on the nations own people. Agent Orange is a defoliant. The military used Agent Orange to strip trees of their leaves in heavily forested areas. Its goal was to deprive enemy fighters of the natural cover provided by the foliage. But what was not discovered until many years later was the high toxicity of Agent Orange to humans. The substance contained dioxin — the same harmful component also created burning trash and fossil fuels.

Because of Agent Orange's high dioxin concentration, many veterans exposed to it later developed severe illnesses. Not just illness, but the leading problems associated with the said agent were Cancer among other body type illnesses.

Concerns that Agent Orange was not just sickening vets but also causing birth defects in their children surfaced after troops returned from war four decades ago. Veterans reported that some of their children had unusual defects — missing limbs, extra limbs and other diseases — that didn't run in their families. Some government studies were done, including Michalek's, but they generally dismissed an association. Recent advances in science, especially in the burgeoning field of epigenetics, have shown that chemical exposure can affect multiple generations. Changes in gene expression — whether a gene for a trait is turned on or off — can be passed from one generation to the next, research shows. A 2012 study, for example, showed that gestating female rats exposed to dioxin, a byproduct found in Agent Orange, passed mutations to future generations.

Many Vietnam veterans, reaching the ends of their lives, are increasingly haunted by thoughts of the full cost of their service. They paid a price, physically, mentally and emotionally, while our government to well knew the seriousness of their chemicals, warfare and effect it would have on anybody around it. Place that into layman's terms and say, they experimented with thousands of people's lives. A health problem that would eventually continue for many decades, and infected people's lives and family.

Blackledge, who fathered a healthy child before the war and two sick ones after, believes the government that exposed troops to Agent Orange should care for those it harmed — including their children.

"I probably wouldn't have had kids," he said, "had I known that there would be an impact on them." Mike Ryan, now 71, said he hadn't kept up with scientific advancements that potentially confirm what he's spent years arguing — that a father's exposure to toxins can cause health problems in offspring. In the end, it won't matter what researchers discover, he insisted.

"They will never admit it," he said, "because if they do, then America is admitting to drafting the unborn."

In 1979, a team of researchers had embarked on a $143 million, 20-year study of those Air Force vets who'd had the greatest exposure to Agent Orange: Those who'd sprayed it. The study was extremely detailed, verifying what veterans said with a host of medical exams and biological specimens, including blood, semen and urine samples. Five years in, Dr. Richard Albanese, a lead investigator, and his team made what they considered an intriguing finding — children born to exposed Air Force vets after the war had more defects than children of those who hadn't handled Agent Orange at all.

The researchers wrote up the results in a report, but their superiors halted its release, saying more research was needed, including physically examining all the children to verify whether they had birth defects, Albanese recalled in a recent interview. After Albanese spoke up about the delay, he was taken off the project and reassigned. The report had all but been forgotten. Deniability was the new plan. The government figured, if they denied any accountability, the said issue would have gone away entirely.

Meanwhile, two major studies from the Centers for Disease Control and Prevention concluded that there was little connection between exposure to herbicides and birth defects. One examined babies born in the metropolitan Atlanta region and found that Vietnam veterans fathered a similar percent of babies with birth defects as other men. A second study compared the rates of birth defects among babies fathered by Vietnam vets to those born to veterans who served elsewhere during the war. Vietnam veterans reported a higher rate of birth defects in their children but that finding was not validated in follow-up reviews of hospital records.

Finally in 1988, under pressure from members of Congress, the study Albanese had worked on was released, but with only his name on it. His study found "a statistically significant increase in reported birth defects" among veterans who handled Agent Orange. Then, four years later, the Air Force published a follow-up paper that claimed no evidence had been found linking Agent Orange exposure to birth defects in the men's children.

The 1992 report looked at the data in a different way. If there indeed was an association, the researchers wrote, they would have expected to find that veterans with more dioxin lingering in their blood would have higher rates of birth defects in their children, but that wasn't the case. They concluded that the few links between dioxin and birth defects "were generally weak, inconsistent or biologically implausible" and the data "provided no support" for such a connection.

These people really bent over backwards to try to disprove a connection," he said. "That's my feeling." Albanese, who now runs a small defense consulting company in San Antonio, said he believes the episode was part of a broader government effort to suppress findings connecting Agent Orange to the health of veterans and their children.

Seven years later, some of Albanese's concerns were investigated by the Government Accountability Office and at a congressional hearing in 2000. The GAO noted the unusual way in which the Air Force report was handled and said one veterans' organization believed it may have delayed the VA's decision to provide benefits to children with spina bifida.

By 1978, Agent Orange and its potential effects had become a national controversy. In response, the VA began offering veterans free examinations and regular notifications when new information about Agent Orange came to light. As part of the effort, information was gathered about each vet and entered into a newly established Agent Orange Registry.

Over the past 18 months, more than 6,000 vets and their family members confronting Agent Orange-related issues have shared their stories with ProPublica and The Pilot. Some said it was inexplicable that VA had collected all their information, then simply stashed it away unexamined.

Schwartz, in a recent interview, said if the U.S. conceded that Agent Orange caused birth defects, the Vietnamese government might seek compensation for children who've been harmed over there. "We ran into a wall," she said. "People were deathly afraid that the Vietnamese would then lodge a horrendous lawsuit against the United States." For now, the VA pays to store the blood, semen and tissue specimens from the former Air Force spray crews in a freezer at a base in Ohio, leaving open the possibility for future studies.

Heather Bowser was born in 1972, three years after her father, William

Morris, returned from Vietnam. His base was less than 10 miles away from Bien

Hoe Air Base, which served as the hub for the Air Force crew that sprayed Agent Orange across the country. The airplanes returning from short missions would often dump Agent Orange in the river alongside his base, he told her.

The fact that our government has had no problems spraying deadly toxins on it's own citizens, is an example of what our government is willing to do. What it is capable of doing any time. The fact that Covid-19 is now killed tens of thousands around the world, It must make some wonder, was this yet another experiment released to see what the worlds population will do when such and chemical agent is released? **Makes one think.**

Operation Ranch Hand was a U.S. military operation during the Vietnam War, lasting from 1962 until 1971. Largely inspired by the British use of 2,4,5-T and 2,4-D (Agent Orange) during the Malayan Emergency in the 1950s, it was part of the overall chemical warfare program during the war called "Operation Trail Dust".

From 1962 to 1971, the U.S. Air Force sprayed nearly 19 million gallons of herbicides in Vietnam, of which at least 11 million gallons was Agent Orange, in a military project called Operation Ranch Hand. An additional quantity (1.6 million gallons has been documented) of herbicides was applied to base perimeters, roadways, and communication lines by helicopter and surface sprayings from riverboats, trucks, or backpacks. Herbicide operations in Vietnam had two primary military objectives: (1) defoliation of trees and plants to improve observation, and (2) destruction of enemy crops. But there was little said about probable side effects and the dangers of the said chemicals when being applied to the average soldier.

# CHAPTER SEVEN

## THE UNITED STATES GOVERNMENT CONDUCTED EXPERIMENTS ON ITS OWN CITIZENS USING AGENT ORANGE CHEMICALS

Throughout history, the US government has managed to keep secrets hidden from the public. When they release these secrets, many are quite surprised and astonished at everything they've managed to get away with.

Countless conspiracies involving programs such as Area 51 and MKULTRA have become mainstream in modern-day culture. The desire for such secretive knowledge is ever abundant, and no matter how much we think we know, we're always proven wrong.

Shocking as it may seem, U.S. government doctors once thought it was fine to experiment on disabled people and prison inmates. Such experiments included giving hepatitis to mental patients in Connecticut, squirting a pandemic flu virus up the noses of prisoners in Maryland, and injecting cancer cells into chronically ill people at a New York hospital.

Despite the current rise in conspiracy theories involving government testing, there are many verified instances of such cases that have remained hidden from the public for decades. The US Public Health Service conducted the Tuskegee Syphilis Study beginning in 1932. A total of 600 African American men were chosen to be involved in the study: 399 with syphilis and 201 without. Those with syphilis were denied proper treatment for the disease; the government wanted to ensure that they were able to track its progression without interruption by medication. The men were never given the option to participate in the study because they were never told it was an experiment.

The experiment was only supposed to last for six months, but it became a long-term study that lasted up to 40 years. When penicillin became the main drug to treat syphilis, the patients were denied access and weren't given the option to opt out of the study. In exchange, they were given free medical exams and burial services. A lawsuit was later filed, and the government granted free burial services to all surviving patients. By offering free burials to the patients or test subjects, they were also able to bury any other evidence of wrong doing.

In the 1940s at Statesville Penitentiary, which is located in xxxxxxxxx was Involved over 400 prisoners who were illegally infected with Malaria and subjected to studies. The goal was to test experimental drugs in an effort to find a cure for the disease. In addition, the tests were administered and documented solely by the prisoners themselves. Not only were they the patients—they were also the proctors. The prisoners also decided which of them would take part in the experiment. The testing process counted toward their sentence and allowed some to serve much less time. The prisoners would also choose who was eligible to receive a reduced sentence. However intriguing this may have been for the prospective patients, the experimental drugs often had irreversible side effects and the prisoners merely ended up losing their own live

One of the most famous prisoners involved in the experiment was Nathan Leopold, who many may recognize from the Leopold and Loeb murder case in 1924. He stated that the prisoners would often deal with the horrifying side effects without complaint. Despite the immorality of this experiment, it was praised by many for the benefits it would create for society. Citizens saw it as a sacrifice to find the cure for Malaria at the prisoners' expense. The prisoners not knowing the exact repercussions from the side effects died with no knowledge and were then used as human guinea pigs. They saw a chance to leave prison early and some did just that. **The only difference was some left in a pine box.**

Edward Cohn, a biochemist working at Harvard University, conducted an experiment in 1942 with sponsorship by the US Navy. The Navy had contacted Cohn to engage in this secret project to discover a possible biological weapon. His work involved injecting prisoners with cow blood in an effort to detect a protein that could be used in the event of an upcoming war. The 64 subjects who were injected with the cow blood all suffered catastrophic effects, ending in death.

Although this government experiment ended in failure, it was soon learned from Cohn's methods that the true way to identify the protein was not in cow blood but in human blood. The methods were replicated using human blood, and the protein was not only isolated, but it was also pure. Instead of being used to harm others, this protein was later used to effectively treat shock patients

In the 1930'sThe Manhattan Project was a research and development program that was undertaking during World War II that produced the first nuclear weapons. It was led by the United States with the support of the United Kingdom and Canada. In 1939, President Franklin Delano

Roosevelt received a letter from physicist Albert Einstein with an urgent message: Physicists had recently discovered that the element uranium could generate vast amounts of energy — enough, perhaps, for a bomb. Einstein suspected that Hitler might already be working to stockpile the element.

Perhaps the biggest experiment known was the Manhattan project, where The United States government did experimentation on its own people. During the mid-1940s, the US was busy with the Manhattan Project, the effort to create the atomic bomb. Because the effects of radiation from the bomb were largely unknown, the government spent years studying them, including with experimentation on its own citizens.

Plutonium is one of the many radioactive materials the government used in these types of tests. Patients would receive doses of radioactive plutonium in the form of injections. A majority of these patients were terminally ill, which made the results of the experiment difficult to fully understand. They were never told what was being done to them, partly because the word "plutonium" remained a government secret until after World War II.

Although most of the patients did not die from effects of the plutonium injections, the government's secrecy and willingness to subject its own citizens to such experiments raised suspicion from many.

U.S. officials also acknowledged there had been dozens of similar experiments in the United States — studies that often involved making healthy people sick. One other incident. A federally funded study begun in 1942 test patients were injected with experimental flu vaccine in male patients at a state insane asylum in Ypsilanti, Mich., whom then were exposed to flu several months later. It was co-authored by Dr. Jonas Salk, who a decade later would become famous as inventor of the polio vaccine.

5 years later the prosecution of Nazi doctors in 1947 led to the "Nuremberg Code," a set of international rules to protect human test subjects. Many U.S. doctors essentially ignored them, arguing that they applied to Nazi atrocities — not to American medicine.

The late 1940s and 1950s saw huge growth in the U.S. pharmaceutical and health care industrie s accompanied by a boom in prisoner experiments funded by both the government and corporations. By the

1960s, at least half the states allowed prisoners to be used as medical guinea pigs

One such study, was that of travesty on children and yet again conducted by our government. At nearby Staten Island, from 1963 to 1966, a controversial medical study was conducted at the Willow brook State School for children with mental retardation. The children were intentionally given hepatitis orally and by injection to see if they could then be cured with gamma globulin.

# CHAPTER EIGHT

## DONALD J TRUMP STOPS FUNDING TO THE WORLD HEALTH ORGANIZATION, FOR COVERING UP CORONA VIRUS SPREAD

Republican senators on Tuesday sent a wide-ranging demand for information, records and documents to the World Health Organization regarding the origins of the novel Coronavirus. It was part of a larger investigation into the global response to the pandemic.

In a letter to Dr. Tedros Adhanom Ghebreyesus, director-general of the WHO, Homeland Security Committee Chairman Ron Johnson, along with Sen. Rick Scott of Florida and a handful of GOP colleagues, requested a sweeping list of materials regarding what they called "WHO's failed and delayed response to the Coronavirus."

Donald J Trump stated "I'm instructing my administration to halt funding of the World Health Organization while a review is conducted to assess the world health organization's role in severely mismanaging and covering up the spread of the Coronavirus," Trump said.

It's a move the president has signaled for weeks as he tries to shift blame for his response to the novel Coronavirus pandemic. The U.S. is the largest donor to the world health agency by far and makes its contribution annually.

While Trump criticized the WHO for what he called a failure "to investigate credible reports from sources in Wuhan that conflicted directly with the Chinese government's official accounts," the president had previously praised President Xi Jinping and China for "their effort and transparency" in handling the pandemic.

Johnson, who launched the investigation with his fellow senators this week, indicated in a Politico interview Monday that although he wanted to mount a sweeping look at the response, including the U.S. government's, the focus of the probe was particularly on the China/WHO component of the crisis.

On Jan. 22, just days after the first positive COVID-19 case surfaced in the

U.S., Trump said he was not worried at all, telling CNBC, "No. Not at all. And we have it totally under control. "at that time the president had merely seen one case in our country, or the United states and had no way of knowing what this pandemic was like, as the at first the Chinese government had did everything in the power, to isolate any suggested media coverage. They lessoned the spread of the virus socially, but in their own country, they had a serious infection problem.

The Johnson letter to WHO — signed by Sens. Kevin Cramer of North Dakota, Martha McSally of Arizona, Steve Daines of Montana, Todd Young of Indiana, and Joni Ernst of Iowa — sought detailed information on protocols and procedures in place at the end of 2019, as a patient in Wuhan, China, tested positive for COVID-19; when the WHO knew of China's first case and when it got boots on the ground there to investigate; who coordinated a response with the ruling Chinese Communist Party; and if the world agency received any "financial compensation outside of their WHO salaries."

The newly-launched Senate inquiry sought agency property, including electronic records, hard drives, emails, and text messages from Oct. 1, 2019, to March 12, 2020.

Scott, a noted China hawk and Homeland Security Committee member, is expected to lead the WHO/China portion of the panel's probe. In a recent Fox News op-ed, the senator made clear his disdain for the WHO which he called a "puppet" and "shill" of Beijing, writing, "American taxpayers are the largest contributor to the WHO budget. There needs to be accountability for their failures and their willingness to help China hide the Coronavirus from the world."

"Whether we cut funding or tie future funding to certain changes in the organization, we have to take action," Scott wrote.

A number of GOP senators supported Trump's recent statements about his administration considering pulling funding from the WHO.

MORE: China rolls out software surveillance for the COVID-19 pandemic, alarming human rights advocates

A spokesman for the Senate Homeland Security Committee was not able to say when the first hearing might take place. The letter requests WHO answers by April 21, and the Senate is not expected to return for business before May 4.

Congressional action could extend beyond the Johnson-Scott probe, with a number of GOP senators calling for retaliatory action against China.

A bill by Sen. Ted Cruz, R-Texas, introduced Tuesday, would impose sanctions on Chinese officials "who engage in censorship through activities that prohibit, limit, or penalize the exercise of freedom of expression or assembly by citizens of the People's Republic of China, including prohibitions, limitations, or penalties related to the use of social media. MORE: Where's the money? Most Americans are still waiting for COVID-19 stimulus boost.

The sanctions are also designed to penalize those Chinese citizens who disseminate inaccurate epidemiological information.

GOP Sen. Josh Hawley of Missouri introduced legislation Tuesday that would "hold the Chinese Communist Party responsible for causing the COVID-19 global pandemic."

The bill would strip the communist country of its sovereign immunity to allow lawsuits and would create a "Justice for Victims of COVID-19 Task Force" at the State Department to lead an international probe of Beijing's handling of the pandemic.

"There is overwhelming evidence that the Chinese Communist Party's lies, deceit, and incompetence caused COVID-19 to transform from a local disease outbreak into a global pandemic. We need an international investigation to learn the full extent of the damage," said Hawley. "The CCP unleashed this pandemic. They must be held accountable to their victims.

As the rest of the world blames the pandemic on China, wading through the recent criteria and said testimonials from prior researchers and scientists that claim seems to be falling short of its mark. It is very easy to accuse and point fingers during any sort of crisis, such as the one we have all been exposed to. I have stated a few different theories, that have raised some desperate concerns. Perhaps this disease we will not know whom did what perhaps the answers lay ahead in a much later time. Whatever the outcome, we as a civilized people need answers and we need them now.

Health officials in Taiwan say they warned the World Health Organization in December 2019 that the Coronavirus could be passed via human-to-human contact, but the organization ignored its warnings, possibly due to its relationship with China, where the virus was suggested it had originated.

The Taiwanese health officials said doctors in the country learned that medical staff on mainland China were getting ill, suggesting human-to-human contact was possible. Officials in Taipei said they reported the information at the end of December 2019. Taiwanese government officials who spoke to the Times said their warnings were not shared by the WHO.

"While the International Health Regulations' internal website provides a platform for all countries to share information on the epidemic and their response, none of the information shared by our country's [Centers for Disease Control] is being put up there," Taiwan Vice President Chen Chien-jen told the Times. "The WHO could not obtain first-hand information to study and judge whether there was human-to-human transmission of Covid-19. This led it to announce human-to-human transmission with a delay, and an opportunity to raise the alert level both in China and the wider world was lost."

Ignoring the fact that early information had been crucial to the seriousness of the Covid-19 virus, In response, the WHO told the Times that it had to "hold frank and open discussions on sometimes sensitive issues" and "respect the confidentiality of such communications."

The largest mistake by the (WHO) World Health Organization at the time, was that they had stated the virus was not spread by human to human contact. The Daily Caller reported that weeks after Taiwan warned them, the WHO on January 14 said the Coronavirus wasn't transferred from human-to-human contact, parroting China's claims at the time. Reuters reported that the WHO downplayed the potential transmission, saying for the first time on that day there may have been human-to-human transmission. On January 15, the head of China's CDC emergency center claimed the risk of human-to-human transmission was "low" thus giving a completely false signal to the entire world.

TECRO noted that the WHO also falsely identified Taiwan as a province of China in its reporting on the Wuhan virus pandemic, which "misled some countries to unjustly mishandle their treatment of Taiwanese passengers or airlines when it comes to border control. That's unfortunate as the politics confuses the international community [on] what's the real and greater interest of international public health." Taiwan, technically the Republic of China, is a sovereign state south of China that has never been part of the People's Republic of China in its history. It is a democratic state with its own military, healthcare system, education system, and diplomatic corps. It receives no financial support and is under no obligation to follow the laws of the Communist Party of China.

Vice President Chen expressed frustration to the Financial Times that Taipei's research on the Wuhan Coronavirus as early as December indicated that the WHO should have begun warning countries at that time of the contagious nature of the virus.

Taiwan reportedly had intelligence on the virus early through doctors in

Wuhan. Scientists have now traced the first known novel Coronavirus case back to

November 17, 2019, documented in the central Chinese metropolis of Wuhan. A University of Toronto study found that warnings from doctors in Wuhan to others that they were facing a new contagious disease began appearing online in December, almost immediately followed by censorship and arrests.

Among the most famous of the eight people first arrested at the time for having "severely disturbed the social order" by warning people to distance themselves and wash their hands was Dr. Li Wenliang, a 34-year-old in Wuhan who died of Coronavirus shortly after being arrested and forced to apologize for posting safety tips on a doctors' on the WeChat group. WeChat is a Chinese Communist Party-approved social media network.

Popular outrage following Li's death resulted in Beijing blaming local Wuhan Communist Party officials for arresting Li and replacing several senior regional officials with loyalists to Chinese dictator Xi Jinping. Some of these warnings reportedly made it to Taiwan, which had built a centralized National Health Command Center (NHCC) to deal with public health crises in the aftermath of the 2003 Sudden Acute Respiratory Syndrome (SARS) viral outbreak. Taiwan rapidly began acting to limit travel into the country from affected areas and put emergency precautions into place. During this time, Taipei also claims to have alerted the WHO, but to no avail. The communists were being silent and so was the WHO. World Health Organization.

With the Chinese governments secrecy and constant misleading of said information, The Communist Party of China shut down a "wet market" in Wuhan – where individuals could freely sell wild animal meat for consumption – on January 1, believing it to be the source of the virus. It made public the existence of a viral outbreak on January 20; subsequent studies have cast doubt on the wet market being the origin of the virus and placed scrutiny on a bio research lab, that is known to have experimented on wild animals bats and other infected animals with similar diseases.

With little or no help from the World Health Organization, On January 14, nearly a week before Beijing revealed the outbreak to the public but nearly two months since the diagnosis of the first Coronavirus case, the WHO said on Twitter, "preliminary investigations conducted by the Chinese authorities have found no clear evidence of human-to-human transmission of the novel #Coronavirus (2019-nCoV) identified in #Wuhan, #China." This created a false front to the American public and people all over the world.

The University of Southampton concluded in a recent study of the the Communist Party of China and stated it could have stopped as many as 95 percent of the world's Coronavirus cases, if it had listened to the instructions of the doctors it silenced and detained in Wuhan.

# CHAPTER NINE

## ELDERLY BODY COUNT CONTINUING AMID CORONA VIRUS CURE

The United States recorded its first Coronavirus fatality on Feb. 29. It took 38 days to reach 10,000 deaths and just nine more days to go from 10,000 fatalities to 30,000. The previous high single-day death toll was 2,364 on Tuesday.

According to the United Nations World Population Prospects report, approximately 7,452 people die every day in the United States. In other words, a person dies in the US approximately every 12 seconds. There are currently 28,579 confirmed deaths surrounding the covid-19 cases and the elderly. There are 1 out of every three persons, who has died whom is between the ages of 54 and 90. As the body counts continue to rise for the second straight day, so do the cases of covid-19 in the elderly homes designated to protecting them In the first big analysis of more than 44,000 cases from China, deaths were at least five times more common among confirmed cases with diabetes, high blood pressure or heart or breathing problems. These are all symptoms that can normally be found in aging and elderly people.

The University Hospital of Wales (UHW) in Cardiff hopes to offer the treatment as part of a study within a month.

Blood will be extracted from people who have recovered from Covid-19 and the plasma will be given to patients.

It is hoped antibodies in the plasma of the blood could help others struggling to fight the infection.

At this early stage, the plan is to trial the treatment on patients who are severely affected by Coronavirus, according to Dr Stuart Walker, medical director at Cardiff and Vale University Health Board.

# CHAPTER TEN

## ANONYMOUS TIP LEADS TO 17 ELDERLY BODIES BEING DISCOVERED IN A MAKE SHIFT SHED

On Wednesday, The New York Times reported that police have found a large number of bodies overloading a small morgue at a nursing home complex in Andover, New Jersey that has been overwhelmed with Coronavirus cases. These types of cases are popping up all across the United States and seem to be in every city and states nursing for the elderly and elderly recovery.

Long term care facility, Andover Subacute care facility has record number of deaths' in one days time and states they had no place to even put the said bodies. Subacute is Andover's largest care facility, housing some 700 patients. Through and anonymous tip police responded, but the nursing home had removed the 17 deceased bodies and had them stored in a mortuary designed to hold no more than three people at one time.

"The 17 were among 68 recent deaths linked to the long-term care facility, Andover Subacute and Rehabilitation Center I and II, including two nurses, officials said," "Of those who died, 26 people had tested positive for the virus. For the others, the cause of death is unknown." but surely attributed to the virus pandemic.

"Of the patients who remain at the homes, housed in two buildings, 76 have tested positive for the virus; 41 staff members, including an administrator, are sick with Covid-19 the disease caused by the Coronavirus, according to county health records shared on Wednesday with a federal official," said the report. "With beds for 700 patients, Andover Sub acute records show, the state's largest licensed facility — and the risk of continued spread is terrifying to family members who have turned to social media and their local congressman, desperate for answers and extra personnel."

There is no question, this virus is and elderly killer, one that seems genetically proofed to attack vital organs such as the upper respiratory system, where mostly the elderly seem to have a very weak immune system. The story below is absolute proof, that the elderly need to be protected at all costs. The truth to the matter, is our nursing homes have almost all been hit with wide casualties from inside each and every one of them. Our elderly are definitely not safe any where they go or reside.

ANDOVER TOWNSHIP — Reports from staff members and family

members who had loved ones become ill and die from the Coronavirus in Andover Rehabilitation and Sub-acute I and II have prompted an investigation, which resulted in the removal of 13 bodies from the Sub acute II facility on Monday.

Lack of staff, PPE, infection control and communications from administration and ownership to staff and families about who has been ill or has succumbed to COVID-19 within the long-term care facilities have been the major complaints from staff and family members. Many have asked where the state or county have been in the midst of the pandemic. complaints over the weekend to the Sussex County Sheriff's Office and Andover Township Police Department have resulted in several investigations at the municipal and county levels of the Andover Sub acute facilities, said Andover Township Police Chief Eric Danielson.

According to Laurie Facciarossa Brewer, the New Jersey Long-Term Care Ombudsman, her office has not had many complaints lodged against the sub acute facilities; but opened three cases for investigation between March 13 and April 13. Her office is unable to visit the facilities during lockdown but said when a complaint is received, residents, and administration and, if necessary, the state Department of Health, are notified.

# CHAPTER ELEVEN

## DEMOCRATS AND SOCIAL MEDIA MISLEADING COVID-19 CASES TO PLACE BLAME ON TRUMP

If anyone suspected there had not been any sort of conspiracy, they need to take a hard look at the facts and then think twice. The simple fact, that the democratic agenda for 4 months, has pushed every single news outlet, every single democratic leader to play the game of let's accuse the president, let's blame him on the outcome and the slower response of this pandemic. Whatever the case, as far as the democrats go, president Trump is guilty of something. This entire idea, has surfaced and people are beginning to believe the democratic party and there leaders and supporters had something to do with this virus. If the goal was to shut down the economy its happened, if the goal was to bankrupt American companies, that has happened or to crash our stalk markets that surely has happened. All these things have hit America and its people hard.

With the democrats and their leaders, seemingly over inflating the said death counts and the media following the same guidelines, we had to wonder, what in the world was the agenda even representing? What benefit would they have to cause a total collapse of our government? That answer might just be somewhat easy to explain. If our economy tanks during trumps presidency, the liberal agenda along with the democratic party can lay blame to our president and sneak in as the next best thing. The fact that the media has been quick to criticize the president even when he clearly has done his job, makes one surmise the agenda is to over throw our government, take out Trump and somehow make America great again the democratic way? It might just be the biggest conspiracy of all. A conspiracy, that may lead to how and why this Covid-19 was released in the first place.

Jordan said Monday on "The Ingraham Angle" that Biden's recent statement that he would use the economic shutdown to push through "green" legislation and initiatives, and House Speaker Nancy Pelosi's, D-Calif., continued public criticism of President Trump while she simultaneously announces that Congress will be out of session until May 4, are examples of how Democrats routinely use a crisis to bolster their political goals. The covid-19 virus is been used exactly in this manner with the failing democratic party.

Jordan also slammed state officials who are using the Coronavirus outbreak to institute draconian orders, often without going through the democratic process of getting a vote from state legislatures. Tucker

Carlson delivered a monologue on how leaders are exploiting the Coronavirus and using it as an opportunity to get their agenda passed. Carlson said Tuesday night that Democrats are using the Coronavirus pandemic to encourage mail-in voting. The FNC host also noted our leaders want mail-in voting and want people to have "immunity papers" to go outside. Some in our political class don't seem sad. For them, this isn't a human tragedy. It's an opportunity. As a rule, it's the most mediocre people who are trying there absolute hardest to exploit the moment. In the long history of the commonwealth of Virginia, it's likely that no politician has ever amassed a record more embarrassing or less impressive than the current governor, Klan-robes Blackface. As the Easter weakened approached, Gov. Klan-robes announced he'd be signing a tall stack of highly radical legislation. Mostly because he could:

Americans aren't locked in their homes, washing their hands, and wondering whether they'll die of pneumonia because all the information they receive from the leftist news sources and social media are accurate.

Rather, hard-left and Democrat activists are pumping out advertisements and faulty "science" to help Democrat president contender Joe Biden and drive public officials to adopt left-wing public policies.

The goals: destroy Trump, elect Biden, and move the country toward totalitarian socialism. That is what seems to me to be a separated conspiracy agenda.

A few key figures you may already have heard about are George Soros A man who collaborated with the Nazis during World War II. Another is leftist billionaire Donald Sussman, the founder of something called New China Capital Management, a major investment outfit. Remember those people, as they are major backers who have all worked with the agendas of the said Democratic Party.

The Democratic Party's largest super PAC — will spend $6 million this week on advertisements criticizing Trump for his response to the Coronavirus pandemic. Regardless if Trump had worked diligently to dispel fears and assist our states governors, the democratic party, is working harder to use the Coronavirus to oust Trump when possible. The ads will run in Florida, Michigan, Pennsylvania, and Wisconsin. The PAC received $3 million in contributions from Soros's Democracy

PAC on Feb. 21, new filings show. Soros's seven-figure donation accounts for 77 percent of the $3.9 million the PAC reported hauling in last month alone.

The PAC will spend $150 million against Trump in key states, Schoffstall reported, and has raised "$27 million since January 2019. Its largest donor has been billionaire hedge fund manager Donald Sussman, who has given the group $8 million this cycle. Soros is now the group's second-largest donor at $5 million."

In its report on the pair of hate-Trump subversives citing the Wall Street Journal, the Media Research Center noted that Sussman gave $21 million to Hillary Clinton's campaign for president, while Soros donated $9.5 million. The former Nazi stooge was Clinton's second biggest contributor.

In final detail "But a closer look at how many of COVID Act Now's predictions have already fallen short, and how they became a ubiquitous resource across the country overnight, suggests something more sinister," Osborn reported: As Americans across the nation began to wonder, just how much of the actual Covid-19 had been misrepresented, even more sinister agendas began to show openly.

The headline of an NBC Oregon affiliate featured COVID Act Now data, and a headline blaring, "Coronavirus model sees Oregon hospitals overwhelmed by mid-April." Both The Oregonian and The East Oregonian also published stories featuring the widely shared data predicting a "point of no return." Michigan Gov. Gretchen Whitmer cited COVID Act Now when telling her state they would exceed

7 million cases in Michigan, with 1 million hospitalized and 460,000 deaths if the state did nothing.

The models predict, ominously, a "point of no return," a great concern because "COVID Act Now's predictions have already been proven to be wildly wrong."

COVID Act Now predicted that by March 19 the state of Tennessee could expect 190 hospitalizations of patients with confirmed Wuhan virus. By March 19, they only had 15 patients hospitalized. In Georgia, COVID Act Now predicted 688 hospitalizations by March 23. By that date, they had around 800 confirmed cases in the whole state, and fewer than 300 hospitalized.

In Florida, COVID Act Now predicted that by March 19, the state would face 400 hospitalizations. On March 19, Gov. Ron DeSantis said 90 people in Florida had been hospitalized.

It's no surprise that COVID Act Now's data are shockingly inaccurate. The people who run the data site are not scientists — meaning virologists or epidemiologists, definitely not scientists.

The founders are Jonathan Kreiss-Tomkins, a Democrat in Alaska's legislature, and three Democrat tech executives: "Zachary Rosen, Max Henderson, and Igor Kofman — who are all also donors to various Democratic campaigns and political organizations since 2016. Henderson and Kofman donated to the Hillary Clinton campaign in 2016, while Rosen donated to the Democratic National Committee, recently resigned Democratic Rep. Katie Hill, and other Democratic candidates."

Conservative talker Rush Limbaugh said during his nationally syndicated radio show on Monday, that "worried" Democrats were using the Coronavirus in an attempt to stop President Donald Trump's campaign rallies. Also implying the stay at home orders were maybe placed in hopes of meddling into Trumps rallies, where he had gained so much support.

One thing for sure is. The Democrats have a coordinated effort underway to attempt to blame the Coronavirus pandemic on President Trump. It's what they do these days – resist and blame everything on the President because that's all they've got. They seek to sow panic and chaos in order to terrorize Americans.

Even before a single case of the virus erupted organically in our country and even as the administration had acted preemptively and effectively to keep virus carriers out of our country, Senate Minority Leader Chuck Schumer, D-N.Y., House Speaker Nancy Pelosi, D-Calif., former New York City Mayor Mike Bloomberg and others were eager to stoke fear and blame Donald Trump. If you did not sense it then, it was really only a matter of time, before people began to realize, there was more to this Covid-19 pandemic. It was as if it was planned and anticipated to hinder the next presidential outcome. All the democrats had to do, was place the blame on Trump and this they have done since the first virus cases.

The Democrats claim that President Trump called the Coronavirus a hoax. As usual, the Democrat-media complex twist his words to serve their political purposes. The reality is that he called the Democrats politicization of the Coronavirus as the new hoax! Those were the actual facts and statements made, not the way the Democrats have stated it. Again if there had been no doubts as to the mission of covid-19,it had also become self evident there is now.

If dealing with the Coronavirus pandemic requires a unified response across the political spectrum. Then the Democrats have offered nothing but a politicization of the situation – even crazily suggesting the virus should be renamed as the "Trump-virus" – tells you everything you need to know about those swishy washy Democrats.

Some are saying that the time line between the Coronavirus and the democratic primaries is somewhat suspicious, as they basically happened around the same time. Many now think, that the entire Coronavirus may have been bought and paid for by the Democratic Party, as one last ditch effort to change this next presidential outcome. If that is so, I would say it is the lowest that anyone could go. Keep in mind, it is the Democratic Party. About the only thing I can say for sure, is if they did not master plan this virus crisis, they definitely have used it to further their said agendas and gain and that is almost as bad.

# CHAPTER TWELVE

## IS THERE A SECRET PLOT TO DAMAGE DONALD TRUMP AND AMERICA?

The debacle began when the U.S. Centers for Disease Control and Prevention (CDC) warned that "disruption to everyday life may be severe" if the disease were to rapidly spread throughout the country. The democrats banked on that said information and then virtually played a role so severe, they scared the entire united States with data, that was not even close to being accurate. One thing for sure, if the democrats lips were moving, they had been telling false truths to the unsuspected catchers, who might just believe it.

What we found, is that the democratic party over a few years now, has done everything in their power to facilitate either a failed economy or completed overthrow of the Republican party and the United States as and entirety, From falsely accusing our president of one matter to the next, to suspected conclusion with Russia. All of which has been cleared and declared and utter waste of time and money spent. So if you follow all the things and barriers thrown at Donald Trump, you should be able to tell, there has been a definite conspiracy against him both in the media and also in our court systems. It is still being played out as the Covid Coronavirus hits its hardest.

And now the highly anticipated Covid-19 virus to offset the campaign trail and mislead the public yet again, is been widely used from every singled democratic governor, to many self inflicting news channels. Reports were being made, that have had no true foundation other than the old "they said it was so".

With Donald Trump growing tired of the constant beat down or alleged beat downs from the conspirators side, the democrats, he began to fight back among the countries most serious crisis. "Tell the Democrat Governors that 'Mutiny On The Bounty' was one of my all time favorite movies," he tweeted. Sending a message, he was ready and willing to handle the covid-19 crisis and the Democratic Party.

A public health crisis is no time for partisanship. Sadly, for the left, they saw the Coronavirus pandemic was just another opportunity for them to take down Trump. From the Russian collusion hoax to the bogus impeachment, they've tried relentlessly to find something to not just damage him, but to end his presidency. The democrats have worked and with all costs to the average American, to use anything they could to derail or end Trumps presidency, so to me it makes sense, that this covid-19 virus may have been their handy work. Or at least they had some sort of hand in the crisis and for their agendas, not anybody else either.

Perhaps one of the biggest and most important tweets, was "In a now-deleted tweet, concerning liberal activist Susan Daniel whom declared, "For the record, if I do get the Coronavirus I'm attending every MAGA rally I can. "with these types of posts and the messages, they have sent, it is ultimately clear there is and agenda, to rid Trump of his presidency, but also to kill any American citizen who opposes what the democratic party has done is doing and will do. It shows the absolute insane levels, they will cross to a point that if we as citizens were not aware, we definitely should be, that there is a conspiracy against anybody not accepting these Democratic baby killers.

It is not just some liberally funded demonstrators claiming the fame of wishing horrific things on people, but also Democratic leaders such as, Denver City Councilwoman Candi CdeBaca, who apparently thought it was appropriate to re-tweet the disgusting comment on her official Twitter account:

The left has made diversity (or lack thereof) a theme of their Coronavirus attacks, taking their Trump Derangement Syndrome to a new level of absurdity. A pandemic is no time for politics. We didn't see Republicans politicize the H1N1 outbreak, but sadly, Democrats have different priorities than the greater good. Democrats are in the middle of a coordinated effort to blame the pandemic on Trump, even though it was congressional Democrats who were distracted by their own efforts to impeach him while the Trump administration was actually doing something about the outbreak.

Mike Bloomberg bought three minutes of airtime to address the public and blame Trump for the outbreak. Both Bloomberg and Joe Biden claimed that the Trump administration cut all budget increases to the CDC and NIH made by the Obama administration, an allegation the Associated Press determined to be false.

With Trump surviving impeachment and the economy booming, the left, desperate to take down Trump, really wanted the public to blame him for the virus, as opposed to, say, China, where it may have originated.

Even though the United States has managed to contain the outbreak better than most countries, that has not stopped Democrats from using the outbreak as an excuse to push their agenda. "When I talk about health care being a human right ... the Coronavirus crisis makes that abundantly clear as to why it should be," Bernie Sanders claimed during his Fox News town hall earlier this month.

Rep. Alexandria Ocasio-Cortez echoed this talking point, claiming the outbreak "absolutely is an argument for Medicare for all."

Except it isn't. As PJM's Tyler O'Neil recently noted, the Coronavirus outbreak actually has proven how socialized medicine has failed countries during this outbreak.

Last week, Joe Biden slammed President Trump's response to the Coronavirus outbreak, calling it a colossal failure. "This virus laid bare the severe shortcomings of the current administration," he claimed, right before explaining what he thought should have been done. Almost point for point, everything that Biden said needed to be done had already been done by Trump. Perhaps one of the worst ways to politicize a crisis is to raise money for your campaign off of it. And that's exactly what Joe Biden did. He sent an email to supporters to read the text of his Coronavirus speech, which blasted President Trump, and included a call for donations at the end of it.

Imagine that. He not only doubled down on his grossly political speech about the Coronavirus, he used it as a call for donations to his campaign. Does it get any worse than that? This is a presidential election season and yes, candidates are free to criticize each other," Karl Rove said in response to these shameful calls for donations. "But should the Democrats' first instinct in a major crisis like

America faces today be to take advantage of the moment for campaign cash?"

# CHAPTER THIRTEEN

## THE HATE AGENDA OF THE FAR LEFT

T he New York Times published an opinion piece by Gerard Alexander, who is an associate professor of politics at the University of Virginia, titled, "Liberals, You're Not as Smart as You Think." The piece is an analysis of how liberals are hurting their own cause by presuming their mental and moral superiority, and thus, are inviting significant backlash against their favored agenda. The prime example is how liberals use their virtual monopoly in the media and the entertainment industry to ruthlessly bash Trump. They're very protective of this monopoly as their goal is ideological segregation. Any signs of diversity of thought are met with disgust and hatred. The most recent example is probably the demonization of Kayne West for his support of Donald Trump.

Keep in mind even Hillary Clinton called us American Trump supporters a basket of deplorables'. With as much anger, as the democratic government has for anybody not voting there ways. One need to keep in mind, that spreading a virus as bad as this is, certainly seems plausible. To be honest I could not place A guarantee, they had not.

Leftists ruthlessly smash their way to ideological purity because they are not prepared to handle any ideas outside their partisan bubble. Diversity of thought is anathema to them, and the strategy they've chosen is to align anything with which they disagree with the worst qualities of humankind. They constantly argue that conservatives should not have the right to voice their opinions. By labeling everyone who disagrees with them a bigot, racist, sexist, etc., they justify discrimination or violence against them. Trump supporters have been assaulted just for being Trump supporters. This isn't just activists on the fringe either. A Manhattan Supreme Court justice recently threw out a case against a New York City bar that had thrown out a Trump hat-wearing customer… for being a Trump supporter. In 2016, a Harvard professor argued that pro-life Christians should be treated like Nazis. The left has failed to recognize that their actions over the past two years are the epitome of the hate they claim to oppose. Either way you see it. **Hate is dangerous to all.**

I am not impressed by way the liberals handled the recent change. One year into the Presidency of Donald Trump, the liberals are still focused on how Donald Trump should have lost the election. A week after the elections, many left wing activists took to the streets to express violence and cause riots all across the nation.

Accusers can paint with very wide brushes. Being a Racist is pretty much the most damning label that can be slapped on anyone in America today, which means it should be applied firmly and carefully. Yet some people have cavalierly leveled the charge against huge numbers of Americans — specifically, the more than 60 million people who voted for Mr. Trump. I am one of those deplorables.

Trump carries a reputation of making deals, and liberals hate it. Liberals speculate if Trump can cut deals with real politicians over real issues? So far in his Presidency, Trump has proven that he is up to that task, even reaching over to the

Democrats to negotiate a deal over DACA (Deferred Action for Childhood Arrivals). Making historic deals concerning trade, the Iran Deal, and other major business deals for companies here in the United States. The biggest obstacle is a healthcare bill aka Obamacare. If Donald Trump can repeal and replace Obamacare, liberals will have no choice but to face embarrassment.

# CHAPTER FOURTEEN

## THE DEMOCRATIC PARTY HAS NO PROBLEMS LINKING ITSELF TO KNOWN URBAN TERRORIST GROUPS

I f you still think that the democratic party could not be responsible for the Coronavirus, guess again. With abortion and baby killing as a chief support for the party, you have to wonder what else they could be capable of. Since the 2016 election Democrats have centered their activism around opposition to President Trump. This furious enmity may have overshadowed some Democrats' friendliness toward Islamic terrorists, and for the Democrat running in California's 50th district it's a family affair.

"Palestinian-Mexican" Ammar Campa-Najjar, also billed as "Latino Arab-American," is the grandson of Yousef al-Najjar, a leader of Black September, the Palestinian terrorist group that abducted, tortured and murdered 11 Israeli athletes at the 1972 Munich Olympics. In 1973, Israeli commandos killed Yousef al-Najjar, and the king of Morocco adopted his son Yasser al-Najjar, who lived in Egypt until 1981 when he reportedly moved to the United States. How Yasser al-Najjar was able to enter the USA remains something of a mystery, but in the official account he married Abigail, a Mexican-American woman, and lived in San Diego, California.

The Democrat now contending with Republican Duncan Hunter, who faces campaign finance violations, claims his father Yasser al-Najjar returned to Gaza in the 1990s to help Yasser Arafat form a government and promote "peace between Israel and the Palestinian people." Yasser al-Najjar served as a de-facto ambassador, defending the Palestinians against charges that they misused money from the government of Norway for anti-Jewish propaganda.

The California Democrat failed to reveal any of this before he launched his campaign. News that Black September terrorist Yousef al-Najjar was his grandfather only emerged in February from the Israeli newspaper Haaretz. The Democrat dismissed it as a "quick take" and said that innocent civilians should never be killed, not quite the same as specifically denouncing the Munich massacre. The terrorist attack also failed to emerge in 2012 when al-Najjar worked in the reelection campaign of POTUS 44.

It was only last June that the "progressive" Democrat legally changed his name from Ammar Yasser Najjar to "Ammar Joseph Campa-Najjar."

This was all of great interest but for establishment media, it was "don't ask don't tell."

For her part, Arizona Democrat Kyrsten Sinema was formerly with the Green Party and made a name for herself organizing rallies against the war in Iraq. In 2003 she promoted events at Arizona State University featuring Lynn Stewart, attorney for terrorist Omar Abdel Rahman. Stewart had been charged with passing messages from Rahman to his terrorist followers.

Rep. Sinema is one of the Democrats who used the services of IT man Imran Awan, who accessed sensitive congressional computers without authorization and destroyed evidence. POTUS 44 judge Tanya Chutkan recently let Awan off with no jail time.

Sinema has equated the deaths of U.S. soldiers in combat with illegal's trying to enter the United States. Republican opponent Martha McSally has charged that Sinema said "it was OK for Americans to join the Taliban to fight against us" and that this was treasonous. Sinema responded that McSally, a U.S. Air Force combat veteran, is "engaging in ridiculous attacks and smearing my campaign. The truth was that this army combat veteran had been doing the right thing and tried to alerting the American voters of what he perceived to be a situation that had serious ties.

Senator Cory Booker Pals With Anti-Israel BDS Terror-Linked Group.8-18-18 We can read the sign: Cory Booker is dumping Israel

As a Democrat with presidential aspirations, it is understandable that Booker wishes to present his bona fides to the rising left-wing of the party. But the senator took the bait when he (wittingly or not) endorsed the pairing of anti-Israel and human-rights causes.

House Judiciary Democrats appear to be all in for protecting left wing terrorism, after their decision to strike down a commonsense proposal to include left-wing terrorism in H.R. 5602, "The Domestic Terrorism Prevention Act of 2020". The amendment, made by Rep. Ken Buck (R-CO), documented dozens of specific violent incidents by left-wing groups or individuals. As the text stands, H.R. 5602's findings mention only right-wing or white supremacist attacks. The legislation does mentions recent anti-Semitic attacks in New Jersey and New York, but fails to mention that perpetrators were reportedly linked to the Black

Hebrew Israelites, a fringe African American group that the FBI has identified as a potential terror risk. This follows on repeated efforts by some on the left -including Congresswoman Rashida Tlaib- to conflate these and similar attacks on Jews in the region with white supremacy, despite the actual identity of the perpetrators.

Although the FBI came under left wing political pressure for highlighting the threat from what they previously termed "Black Identity Extremists." The FBI now prefers the term "Racially Motivated Extremism," which includes both Black and White supremacist groups.

This latest move made by House Democrats shows once again how fundamentally dishonest and unserious the discussion of domestic terrorism has become. While Republicans are willingly to admit that there is some level of threat from violent white supremacists -acknowledging that it is a threat among several significant domestic terror threats- the left continues to ignore and dismiss any and all threats except those they can exploit for political advantage, even if that requires mislabeling incidents and eliminating references to terror threats that originated from other groups.

Sen. Cotton has warned for weeks that the Chinese Communist Party conspired to conceal the true provenance of its virus and the pandemic it spawned. That's no longer a "theory." It's a fact. So, apparently, is the conclusion that the CCP virus came out of a laboratory in Wuhan, not some nearby "wet market."

Now, the so-called "smart people" insist that the virus that came from the PRC lab was not engineered to be a biological weapon. We'll see. What's no conspiracy theory is that the Chinese Communists have an illegal biological warfare program and that they have learned much about its utility from the damage the CCP virus has done to America. Whatever the said case, this biological weapon has done two primary things, one it has caused world panic and two, it has also caused an economic collapse of the entire world. If anyone ever would have surmised that the elderly would have any type of comfortable living, they need to reevaluate that thought. I say this based on the reported deaths of our elderly worldwide.

Ever since the news about the Coronavirus was picked up by global media, speculations about the communist government of China trying to 'cover-up' the outbreak and hide the official figures were rife. The fact that the Chinese Government tried to suppress the attempts of the whistleblowers (the insiders as well as eight doctors), who tried to warn the public of the pandemic, is rather alarming and didn't help their cause.

The alleged Canadian 'policy breach', highlighted the bio-weapon program of other countries including China. Dr Francis Boyle, the creator of Bio Weapons Act, also claims that 'the Coronavirus is an offensive biological warfare weapon with DNA-genetic engineering'. I myself along with millions have been saying this since the beginning of this virus. Do not forget millions of us were sick with something different, that had hit hard in January of this year. Doctors stated it was a bad flu season without doing a lot of testing.

Even though the claims of this pandemic as being a biologically engineered virus, are unsubstantiated, it does not mean, that it has not been proven as an accident either. Scientists haven't been able to determine the origin of COVID-19 but speculations are rife that the virus originated in the seafood market. This was substantiated by reports from Chinese health authorities and the World Health Organization which said that "most" cases had links to the seafood market, which was closed on 1 January.

Skeptics' on the online forums, however, have been sharing suspicions that the virus could have originated from Wuhan, Institute of Virology, which houses China's only level- four bio-safety laboratory (the highest-level classification of labs that study the deadliest viruses).

The institute is said to be the nation's only Biological Security Level 4-certified lab, the highest level in the hierarchy of bio-safety and bio-containment procedures codified by the US Center for Disease Control and Prevention. The Wuhan lab has the equipment and staff to handle the most infectious viruses, including Ebola. There is no secret, that Communist China has been diligently working on weapons of mass destruction and this deadly disease Covid-19.

Republican Indiana Rep. Jim Banks warned of the impending Coronavirus pandemic days as far back as January. The lawmaker credited his foresight to his ongoing focus on China's human rights violations and the country's pattern of misinformation and propaganda.

He credited his foresight to his ongoing focus on China as a threat to national security, an area that he said other lawmakers would do well to focus on.

Richard Ebright, a biology professor at Rutgers University in New Jersey, told the BBC that genomic sequencing of the Coronavirus showed no proof that it had been artificially modified, yet he could not rule out the possibility that the unfolding pandemic could be the result of a "lab incident. " Now given the fact that the virus is said to be a combination or mixture of Sars, there is little doubt also to think, it was nothing short of bio chemical warfare and that it was released upon all of us worldwide. The said virus was aimed to do one main thing, kill as many people around the world, as it could. It just so happened to be the elderly and aging, that became the most infected by the attacking deadly disease.

# CHAPTER FIFTEEN

## THE MORE WE KNOW, THE LESS WE KNOW

According to Douglas Adams' his book, "the answer to all the ultimate questions of life", the universe, and everything else, in reality isn't so uncomplicated. Many experts have compiled significant research on how the universe began, how it works, and what it is. It appears to be a never ending story. The more we learn about the universe, the more questions arise. Experts such as Albert Einstein "the more I learn, the more I realize how much I don't know", and Socrates "I know that I know nothing" have pointed this out.

There is one thing we do know, our world is getting more complicated all the time. As recently as the 20th century people only had a black and white television with one or two senders; there are now over a hundred senders you can choose from. Not to mention all the additional options like cable TV, HD, Netflix, cinemas and many, many more. Between black and white there are now over fifty shades of grey and billions of different colors- literally, for television, but also figuratively, for life in general. As the world around us becomes more complex, the amount that we can really understand about it decreases. Even experts agree on knowing too little, it's no surprise that information overload gives millennial's stress and difficulty to make decisions it is called (choice overload).

As we take a close look at this pandemic and world wide spread of a bio weapon so dangerous, that the elderly must remain locked in their homes. We now must ask questions, that most likely by our own government and world governments, will surely go unanswered. Is the Chinese government hiding information and/or dispensing disinformation? Did the Chinese government create the actual virus in a Chinese biological warfare laboratory? Did the virus come from a Chinese food and seafood market in Wuhan Province? Did Patient One eat a bat, a snake or a pangolin (armored anteater) and thus the virus transmitted from the flesh of an animal into a human being, morphing along the way? those are questions you will need to seek and find and answer by your selves.

This would not be the first time that the Chinese government officials have misrepresented the truth. Since the inception of the People's Republic of China in 1949 under the leadership of Chairman Mao Zedong, official Chinese government propaganda is as common as wonton soup with a side order to fried rice.

A respected international journal, Foreign Policy, had a headline on their January 29, 2020 website stating, "The Wuhan Virus Is Not a Lab-Made Bio-weapon." However, just days later on February 3, 2020, the same journal's website stated, "Chinese Officials can't help lying about the Wuhan Virus."

The deceased whistleblower ophthalmologist, Dr. Li Wenliang, wrote the following social media post to a class of his Wuhan medical students on December 30, 2019: "Seven cases of SARS (Severe Acute Respiratory Syndrome) have been confirmed in the South China fruit and seafood market . . . they were isolated in the emergency department of our hospital."

(Source:).


Dr. Wenliang died of the corona virus weeks later. Another rumor that seems to be in question, is did the Chinese government intentionally infect him? Did they kill him, before he could spill information that the Chinese government was working so hard to seal off? We may never know.

If you had any suspicion, that this virus was not manufactured by communist China, then ask yourselves. What of the other physicians who were silenced by the Chinese government? And also ask why has the government delayed the arrival of researchers and doctors from the World Health Organization (W.H.O.)? Not only blocking but now keeping the investigation by the Corona Task Force, from gaining valuable answers. If there was no government conspiracy, there sure as hell is now.

Also, a paper that appeared in the prestigious medical journal The Lancet at the end of last month has lent credibility to speculation about the origins of the virus. The paper quoted seven doctors at Wuhan's Jinyintan Hospital as saying that the first patient admitted on December 1 had "never been to the wet market," nor had there been any epidemiological link between the first patient and subsequent infection cases, based on the data from the first 41 patients treated there. Furthermore, a note from the Chinese Ministry of Science and Technology is seen as a tacit admission that some kind of incident may have occurred at the Wuhan lab. Not at the Chinese Wet Market.

Meanwhile, Hong Kong's Ming Pao daily reported on Monday that the CCDC had sounded the alarm in a report on the emerging SARS-like outbreak submitted to the top leadership in early January. However, curbing the spread was not at the top of the agenda when Xi and other members of the party's upper echelon sat down for a meeting on January 7. Citing its source, the broadsheet said top leaders were opposed to any contingency measures "that may mar the festive vibe and make the public panic." Instead the United States government and Chinese leaders all kept the pandemic as secret for as long as they could.

Remembering the report of Chinas dangerous lab conditions from 2018. The United States government, also had been working hard to conceal the said report. The government kept the lab report as a classified document, so it could be kept secret from journalists and the main stream media. Back in 2018, the lab had been officially declared as being unsafe and not up for support of being a non threat to national security. With the said report being that poor, one should want to know why there was nothing done then to warn anybody. Why wasn't and alarm sounding off to expose the fact, that billions of lives could be affected. The old saying holds true. **The more we know, the less we know!**

I would like to think, that by the main stream media telling us about the Corona virus, it would cause a bad ripple of worldwide panic. I would like to think, that was why our government had been so secretive. With the way that the media, has what I feel over played this pandemic, the secretiveness by the government was not to scare the public, but instead to conspire against us in ways we simply cannot understand. Since 2018,absolutely no measures had been taken to get more ventilators, gloves and masks and equipment needed in cases such as this last covid-19 outbreak. Nothing had been done, even since the SARS outbreak. Call it a lack of either caring, or a deliberated attempt to cause harm and disarray of world order. **I would like to call it total governmental conspiracy and their secrecy.**

# CHAPTER SIXTEEN

## THE FOOD SUPPLY CUT SHORT AMONG RISING COVID-19 CASES

If you had thought the death count and infected case overload was bad, now we are having to deal with the food situation and the probability, that a war on our agricultural needs may be under attack. In the past few days, more television hype from various news sources, has spoken of meat processing plants that have had to close. Two plants that process Pork and one of the largest chicken processing plants, had to stop operations in lieu of covid-19.

Across the country, major meat processors are starting to shut down plants as employees are getting infected by Coronavirus. Tyson, one of the world's largest meat processors, suspended operations at its Columbus Junction, Iowa, pork plant this week after more than two dozen workers contracted Covid-19 there.

The Coronavirus pandemic has forced one of Canada's major beef processing plants to shut down, with no estimated date of reopening, as cattle producers warn they could lose $500 million over the coming weeks. The Cargill meat processing plant in High River, Alta. temporarily closed Monday after the operation was linked to more than 350 cases of COVID-19 in the suburban community outside Calgary.

The company said it typically processes 4,500 cattle per day, which the Canadian Cattlemen's Association says represents 36 per cent of the country's beef production capacity. The company said there is no scheduled date for the facility to resume production, and that workers will continue getting paid according to their collective bargaining agreement.

In Kansas, Gov. Laura Kelly sent personal protective equipment and testing supplies to counties with meat processing plants. Gov. Kristi Noem said she didn't think it would be difficult to fulfill federal requirements to reopen a shuttered facility in South Dakota. And Iowa Gov. Kim Reynolds warned of the dire cost of closing plants, even as she acknowledged the certainty of more clusters of infection at the facilities.

JBS USA said Monday it was suspending operations at a large pork processing plant in southwestern Minnesota because of an outbreak of COVID-19 among workers — the latest facility to be closed in the public health crisis. Minnesota Health Commissioner Jan Malcolm said 33 JBS employees and six close relatives had tested positive as of Saturday.

Iowa's governor has also warned of the threat to food supply if authorities clamp down too hard on facilities with outbreaks, and has refused to shutter a sprawling Tyson Foods pork processing facility in Waterloo where dozens of workers are infected.

Just today The United Nations made it perfectly clear as the world is dealing with the Coronavirus pandemic, it is also "on the brink of a hunger pandemic" that could lead to "multiple famines of biblical proportions" within a few months if immediate action isn't taken. First of all I would like to know what that action is supposed to be.

The world Food Program Executive Director, David Beasley told the U.N. Security Council that even before COVID-19 became an issue, he was telling world leaders that "2020 would be facing the worst humanitarian crisis since World War II." That's because of wars in Syria, Yemen and elsewhere, locust swarms in Africa, frequent natural disasters and economic crises including in Lebanon, Congo, Sudan and Ethiopia, he said.

But he said he raised the prospect of "a hunger pandemic" because "there is also a real danger that more people could potentially die from the economic impact of COVID-19 than from the virus itself." The WFP chief said lockdowns and economic recession are expected to lead to major income losses for the working poor.

# CHAPTER SEVENTEEN

## THE (C.D.C) CENTER FOR DISEASE CONTROL NOW SAYING EXPECT DECEMBER TO EVEN BE WORSE THAN CURRENT PANDEMIC

If the rising amount of deaths around the world, are not enough to worry about, here comes even worse news. Most may not be ready for. Even as states move ahead with plans to reopen their economies, the director of the Centers for Disease Control and Prevention warned Tuesday that a second wave of the novel Coronavirus will be far more dire because it is likely to coincide with the start of the flu season.

I just can't understand, how anybody can predict something that they claim to know nearly nothing about. How is it, that when the government needs to tell the world about something, even after they openly say we do not know enough about this pandemic, but on the other hand, they say and can make predictions? all the sudden they are the seeing eye and know everything?

"There's a possibility that the assault of the virus on our nation next winter will actually be even more difficult than the one we just went through," CDC Director Robert Redfield said in an interview with The Washington Post. "And when I've said this to others, they kind of put their head back; they don't understand what I mean. To be honest I am sure nobody knows what he means.

In a wide-ranging interview, Redfield said federal and state officials need to use the coming months to prepare for what lies ahead. As stay-at-home orders are lifted, officials need to stress the continued importance of social distancing, he said. They also need to massively scale up their ability to identify the infected through testing and find everyone they interact with through contact tracing.

Doing so prevents new cases from becoming larger outbreaks.

As part of the White House guidelines released last week for a gradual reopening of the country, testing by CDC teams is already underway in nursing homes in four states for asymptomatic cases. The four states are Nebraska, New Mexico, North Dakota and Tennessee.

The CDC has about 500 staff in the states working on a variety of public health issues, and most will pivot to the covid-19 response, Redfield said. The CDC also plans to hire at least another 650 people as experts to "substantially augment" public health personnel in the states and assist with contact tracing, among other tasks, he said. Another wards, now that our government may have infected us, they want to now document and spy on those, who have tested positive or have had the said virus themselves? They call it mapping. I call it as I see it, so they know whom to infect with the antibodies or said vaccine, is what they are really saying and doing.

At least two people who died in early and mid-February had contracted the novel Coronavirus, health officials in California said Tuesday, signaling that the virus may have spread and been fatal in the United States weeks earlier than previously thought. This theory based on new evidence suggested, that the original mapping of the said virus pandemic and suggested exposure, had probably happened maybe even months before the first case had been reported. This report suggests one theory, was that the virus actually did happen before or around January, as previously thought.

If the C.D.C. is correct, as they have openly supported the just station period of the corona virus to be 14 days, it means than that the virus had been around as early as December of 2019. With now conflicting reports of people being carriers of the disease, that have no known illnesses, it is even further easy to believe that the Covid-19 virus may have been around infecting people for months prior to the first reported cases.

Chapter18age99. Millions now hungry and unemployed.

A further 4.4 million Americans sought unemployment benefits last week as the economic toll from the Coronavirus pandemic continued to mount. With current statistics more than 26.6 million now unemployed and going hungry and With so many Americans filing emergency unemployment, due to the Coronavirus, the states computerized unemployment system, has been plagued with problems. Millions have stated they cannot even get on the site to file unemployment. let alone report as directed by the unemployment's guidelines.

Economists have warned that the world is facing the sharpest slowdown since the Great Depression in the 1930s. In the US, the economy is expected to contract 5.9% this year, according to the International Monetary Fund. In just five weeks, the surge in unemployment claims has exceeded the number of jobs created in the near-decade of expansion that ended in February.

Even though the president had stated that they were bailing out small businesses, they are not getting their money promised to them.

A \$349bn relief package programmed for small businesses, part of the \$2tn rescue legislation, ran out of funds within two weeks. Reviews have found that roughly two-thirds of the money so far has gone to large publicly listed companies rather than mom-and-pop shops. Firms with pre-existing relationships with banks, whom typically have larger businesses, were at an advantage.

# CHAPTER EIGHTEEN

## MILLIONS NOW HUNGRY AND UNEMPLOYED

Even if jobless claims continue to subside as reopening gets underway, analysts say the scars on America's consumer-driven economy will linger. The head of the U.N. food agency warned Tuesday that, as the world is dealing with the Coronavirus pandemic, it is also "on the brink of a hunger pandemic" that could lead to "multiple famines of biblical proportions" within a few months if immediate action isn't taken.

NEW YORK: American families have been slammed by the Coronavirus pandemic and are turning more and more to food banks to get by, waiting hours for donations in lines of cars stretching as far as the eye can see. And with 22 million plus people out of work, they are all seemingly overnight as business after business closes under the Great Lockdown. These charities feeding the said hungry and scared people, have one thing in common, that fear the day will come when they cannot cope with the tsunami of demand.

All over America, from New Orleans to Detroit, people abruptly stripped of a paycheck are flocking to food banks - sad scenes of desperation among people waiting for their small share of stimulus money included in the US$2.2 trillion emergency relief package approved by Congress last month.

Perhaps the most dramatic picture of some Americans' new food insecurity unfolded April 9 in San Antonio, Texas, where a staggering 10,000 cars showed up at one food bank, with some families arriving the night before to just sit and wait. To sit and hope, they will be able to get food to survive. To me the biggest question I should be asking is, why the federal government has not shipped food by way of trucks to areas that simply don't have jobs, money for food and are utterly just plain hungry.

After a month of all this frenetic work, the food banks are holding up, at least for now. But the future like for so much of the new world created by the pandemic is uncertain.

# CHAPTER NINETEEN

## THE AGING NOW HAVE NO PLACE TO GO

The first major outbreak of COVID-19 in the nation was at the Kirkland Life Care Center in Washington state. In January, 911 calls began rolling in from the center. Those at Kirkland discovered that the virus was very difficult to contain. In a few short weeks, 37 lives were lost, an early sign of what was to come in similar facilities around the nation.

If anybody had ever surmised there would be attacks on our elderly, it was right when the calls came in and health officials were being alerted as to the seriousness of the Coronavirus. The suggested first cases in Kirkland, represented a small sign, that our elderly were unsafe and in imminent danger to an unseen enemy. An enemy, that certainly hunted the elderly down and stalked them with no remorse.

With the elderly death count climbing just in the United States alone, it has surpassed the ten thousand plus range, they now have no safe place to live and no place to go. As nursing homes now see a spike in the infected and dead, they have been overwhelmed with Corona virus patients. The number of nursing home residents who have succumbed to the novel Coronavirus in the United States has surpassed 10,000, a new survey of state data compiled by ABC News has found. This surge in deaths, accounting for about 40% of all Coronavirus fatalities in the nation, comes as nursing homes across the country continue to struggle for effective strategies to fight the virus, which can quickly overwhelm the communal settings once it enters.

There have been at least 10,631 deaths of long-term care residents, but there are likely many more. The statistics were compiled using official data from states' departments of health and governor's offices in 28 states and the District of Columbia, with the other states not yet reporting the numbers or not responding to requests for the information.

Earlier this week, the leaders at the Centers for Medicare and Medicaid announced they would begin requiring nursing care facilities to report cases of COVID-19 directly to health officials there and at the Centers for Disease Control and Prevention. So far, neither agency has released comprehensive national data on nursing home cases or fatalities during the outbreak.

With so many elderly and aging and them already having health problems, this virus has been labeled the blame of the elderly patients passing, often times when they do die from other causes. This is been a serious problem, because the coroners are not able to do many autopsies and the curious thing, is that the bodies are always being cremated without any proper identifications as to why they died. Family members, their loved ones should have the right to know what happened, how they died and so forth.

As the death count rises, some critics have called on the Trump administration to focus more attention on the long-term care facilities where the virus has been claiming some of the nation's most vulnerable residents........ the aging and elderly.

The Canterbury Rehabilitation Center in Virginia where COVID-19 would go on to claim the lives of 49 residents, health officials looked to the Kirkland Life Care Center, where the first suggested cases were for guidance on how to manage outbreaks in elder-care facilities. But Virginia health officials said they failed to anticipate the potential for the virus to spread between residents who were not showing symptoms of infection.

In early March, the Health administration expanded warnings to nursing homes across the country to begin screening visitors for possible respiratory illnesses. However they did not have enough evidence or information, at that time to self diagnose people. Some people had no symptoms, no fevers or coughing and had displayed no signs, they were infected. It was not until march, when the C.D.C came out and notified us people could have the virus and give it to others.

# CHAPTER TWENTY

## WAS THE CORONA VIRUS DEVISED TO COST TRUMP THE ELECTION?

W hite voters, especially the elderly, gave Donald Trump the U.S. presidency in 2016. But might fail to deliver the same result Nov. 3. One reason, is it seems according to a recent study and said report. A surprising study says 11,000 more Republicans than Democrats, 65 years of age and older, in both Michigan and North Carolina might die before the Nov. 3 elections. According to this report all republican states has seen a larger number of republican deaths, then democratic voters.

If anybody had surmised, that this virus was planted in time to derail a presidential victory, they could be right. The reason I say this, is because the COVID-19 pandemic was tearing through the country is killing-off a disproportionate percentage of the elderly white Republicans that voted Trump into office four years ago. In the U.S. and around the world, most of those who die from the Coronavirus are older persons, mainly men, 60 years-old and above. Trump supporters for the most part.

In 2016, 51% of voters with ages from 50- to 64-year-old's whom voted for Trump while 53% of those were 65 and older. Whites accounted for nine-in-ten (88%) of Trump's supporters as against 60% that voted for Hillary Clinton.

Clinton's voters were younger than Trump's on average (48% were younger than

50 compared with 35% for Trump

# CHAPTER TWENTY-ONE

## CORONA VIRUS TARGETS TRUMP VOTERS AGED 53 TO 80

I hope I am wrong about this, however if the reports are accurate. It could change the presidency. In A published academic report contends the massive case and death toll being inflicted on Americans by the raging COVID-19 pandemic stands to strongly alter the political landscape in battleground states such as Florida, Michigan, Pennsylvania, and Wisconsin. These massive demographic shifts should be enough to give former vice president Joe Biden the presidency.

Data compiled by U.S. Centers for Disease Control and Prevention (CDC) reveals eight-in-10 Coronavirus-related deaths in the U.S. have been among people ages 65 and older. The share of people in the oldest age brackets is larger in the U.S. than in most other countries. This means 11% of people in the U.S. are 70 or older compared with 6% worldwide. Also, 7% of people in the U.S. are 75 or older compared with 3%, while 4% are 80 or older (compared with 2%).

So after seeing the statistics, either this virus pandemic was a deliberate bio weapon created in a Wuhan laboratory, or a virus so complex, it manifested from three different animals. I think, as they say, there is something fishy in both The United States and China and is Perhaps the greatest conspiracy of all times.

**One thing to say, is that as the entire world watches on desperately needing answers, we all share the pain, sympathy and regret of allowing our government to control and manipulate us, as we live our daily lives.**

**"I would like to say "The End" but I fear this might be**

The **Beginning."**

# ABOUT THE AUTHOR

My name is E. Lee. Jensen. I am A blogger, writer and former talk radio show host and radio producer of several shows. I have done well over a hundred interviews from various shows, both on the internet and on F.M radio airwaves. I have a loving daughter and have been married over 26 years. We reside now in Washington State.